An Exquisite Corpse

Death in Surrealist New York

Helen A. Harrison

To Roy
Always

This is a work of fiction, in which historical figures and invented
characters interact. Some of the events described actually happened;
others are pure fantasy, products of the author's imagination.

Published by Mira Digital Publishing
Printed in the United States of America

ISBN 978-1-63110-245-5
Library of Congress Control Number: 2016911202

Man Ray, André Breton, Yves Tanguy and Max Morise, *Exquisite Corpse*, 1928
Pen and brown ink, graphite with smudging, and colored crayons
on cream wove paper. 12 ¼ x 7 ¾ inches
The Art Institute of Chicago. Lindy and Edwin Bergman Collection, 106.1991
© 2016 Man Ray Trust / Artists Rights Society (ARS), New York / ADAGP, Paris

In the Surrealist parlor game *exquisite corpse*, artists build a figure on an absurd assembly line. Typically a piece of paper is folded into sections and passed around; the challenge is that each artist must work on one particular segment without having seen the others. The results are often monstrous, or at least mismatched.

—*The New York Times*, March 29, 2012

Saturday night, October 16, 1943

ONE.

André Breton did not need to examine the body to determine that his friend was dead. His work as a medic on the front lines during the Great War had taught him all he needed to know about corpses. There were no visible wounds or blood, but the skin had lost its coppery glow and faded to a yellowish gray. Although he realized there would be no pulse, he removed his glove, bent down and touched his fingertips to the neck. The flesh was cool, but the muscle was pliant. No rigor.

Breton was not squeamish—his experience in the trenches had taken care of that—yet the sight of Wifredo Lam sprawled on the floor of his studio both saddened and appalled him. As fellow Surrealists forced into exile from Hitler's Europe, they had been on the run together, and as refugees in New York they were outsiders marking time until the Nazis were driven out of Paris and they could return. Their bond had been strengthened by this shared peril and displacement, and Breton's sorrow was deepened by the knowledge that Lam would not live to reclaim his honored place among the Parisian avant-garde.

As if that were not enough, he also had to reckon with the condition of the body.

Lam lay on his back. Over his handsome face, a grotesque African mask stared up from the floor. One outstretched arm was stuffed into the folds of an umbrella, and the other sported a galosh. A large rubber chicken claw covered his left foot. His right trouser leg was rolled up to the knee, leaving his lower leg and foot bare.

Breton knew exactly what he was looking at.

An exquisite corpse.

Clearly the next step was to report it to the police, but he hesitated for two reasons. He spoke virtually no English, and he doubted that he would find a French-speaking person in a Greenwich Village police station. Even if he could make them understand that there was a dead body in an apartment on West 10th Street, how would he explain the bizarre costume? He knew its meaning, but only a Surrealist would appreciate the significance. And no one but a Surrealist would have decorated the body that way, which strongly suggested that the killer was a member of his immediate circle.

Breton wasn't ready to face that possibility alone. With a gloved hand, he turned off the studio light. In the kitchen, Lam's keys were hanging on a nail. He took them, locked the apartment door behind him, and went to find a translator.

TWO.

When Breton arrived at Roberto Matta's building, in the quaint residential alley known as Patchin Place, the outside door had been left open, as was the door to Matta's apartment, where a party was in full swing. The living room rug had been rolled away, and two couples, William and Ethel Baziotes and Gerome and Marianna Kamrowski, were dancing to Glenn Miller and his orchestra, live on CBS Radio. Breton thought he might find his wife, Jacqueline Lamba, whose English was quite good, but she was not in evidence. Under the pretext of renewing the canapé tray, she and her young lover, David Hare, had retreated to the privacy of the kitchen, where they were renewing their acquaintance with each other's bodies.

The place was thick with smoke, under which the smell of oil paint was detectible. Matta had left the studio door ajar so his guests would be sure to see and admire his latest work. He was in there now, soliciting the thoughts of Mercedes Matter—a fellow artist as renowned for her beauty as she was respected for her neo-Cubist paintings, her discerning eye, and her outspoken opinions—whom he was also trying hard to seduce. They both spoke fluent French, and in fact they were flirting in that language, with Matta using the similarity of their names to suggest that a merger was appropriate. Breton was too discreet to interrupt.

He scanned the room for other Francophones, hoping to see Robert Motherwell, the self-appointed American ambassador to the European expatriate community. With his innate distrust of authority, especially the police, Breton would have preferred a native English speaker, someone familiar with the local system, but apparently Motherwell had skipped the party. He noticed Djuna Barnes, the eccentric lesbian author who lived in the upstairs apartment. He was surprised to see her, as she was becoming more and more reclusive since her forced return to her native country. They had known each other in Paris, where she was a fixture of the vanguard literary scene in the 1920s, but with virtually no audience here for her work she was being supported by the heiress Peggy Guggenheim, a collector of art and artists, who had also returned reluctantly from her bohemian expatriate life in Europe. It was evident that Barnes had had plenty to drink, so Breton ruled her out.

Using the only armchair as a de facto throne, the writer Harold Rosenberg was holding court, his high-pitched voice cutting through the music and the chatter. His bad leg, the result of osteomyelitis, kept him off the dance floor, and he used it as an excuse to station himself where others would have to come to him. He was surrounded by a trio of muses—his wife, May Tabak, and the artists Lee Krasner and Elaine Fried—encouraging his philosophizing.

While keeping up a lively banter with Harold, Lee had one eye on her lover, Jackson Pollock, sitting by himself in a corner, studying his shoes and nursing a glass of dago red. She was rationing him, and wanted to be sure he wasn't cheating. He had an important exhibition coming up in just a few weeks, and he couldn't afford any time off for a bender.

Lee was becoming a bit weary of Harold's pontificating. She would have enjoyed dancing, but no partners were available. Dancing with Jackson was out of the question. Their one and only attempt had been a disaster. Of course he had been stinko, cut in on her boyfriend Igor, stepped all over her feet, and propositioned her. Not the most promising start to a romantic relationship—she hadn't spoken to him again for five years—but when she saw his astounding paintings all was forgiven. In fact she fell in love with his art first, then with him.

"The Europeans are completely justified in thinking that the term 'American culture' is an oxymoron," Rosenberg asserted with customary assurance. "Whoever said America's only contribution to civilization is indoor plumbing forgot that the Romans invented it two thousand years ago. Everything we have that's worthwhile in art, science, literature, you name it, is imported from Europe."

Lee was not ready to accept such a dismissive attitude. "Come off it, Harold. If European culture is so superior, why is it destroying itself as we speak? Or rather, as you speak," she added, "since no one else has been able to get in a word for the past half hour."

Rosenberg carried on unfazed. "What's happening now is anti-cultural," he argued. "The Nazis and the Fascists can't tolerate anything but their own warped ideology. Their lust for power is inflamed by profiteers who buy political influence, and by their lackeys in the military. What chance do the poets and painters have against such evil greed? That's why the great minds of Europe are here in New York. They're our most valuable imports.

"Look at the Surrealists," he continued. "They witnessed firsthand what the last war did to their society, and they rejected the values that fostered destruction instead of creation. They chose to be outcasts because they had nothing to lose."

"They didn't invent iconoclasm," countered Elaine. "Every culture has its innovators. And it's only natural that they would look inside themselves for inspiration when what's outside is such a mess. It's terrific that so many Surrealists are here now, that they have a safe place to hide from Hitler, but they had already made their advances long before they got here."

Invoking her lover, the painter Willem de Kooning, she added, "Bill says they're running out of creative juice because New York is more surreal than anything they could dream up."

This exchange would have infuriated Breton if he had been able to understand it. But his lack of English was the very reason he was absorbed in his search for a translator. He spotted Marcel Duchamp, engrossed in a chess game with de Kooning. Oblivious to the hubbub around them, both artists were capable of focusing their concentration to neutralize distractions. Duchamp was now Breton's objective, and he made straight for him.

"Mon cher Duchamp," he interrupted, "un moment, je t'en prie."

It took a few seconds for Duchamp to re-focus. Breton's voice sounded anxious, and that got his attention. "What is it, my friend?" he replied. They conversed in French.

"I have just come from Lam's. There is a problem, and I need your help."

"What is wrong?" asked Duchamp. "You look distraught."

"Please come with me. I will explain on the way."

Duchamp rose from the table, politely excused himself to de Kooning, retrieved his coat and hat from the bedroom and left with Breton.

10

Taking the seat vacated by Duchamp, Elaine wondered aloud what Breton was up to. "Why the rush to leave? He wasn't here five minutes. And why did Duchamp go with him? Didn't he give you a clue?"

De Kooning shrugged. "Not a visper."

THREE.

As they made their way to Lam's apartment, Breton explained that his job as a broadcaster for the Voice of America's European service had kept him late at the radio studio on West 57th Street. In those days of military stalemate for the Allies on the Western front, and the Nazis' increasing stranglehold on occupied France, his famous voice helped reassure his countrymen that they had not been abandoned in favor of the liberation of North Africa and Italy.

The work was simple—he didn't have to write the morale-boosting propaganda he read—but he did have the option to revise and approve it and to contribute his own scripts if he wished. The whole process was emotionally exhausting. Even though his words were addressed to nameless, invisible listeners, they brought back memories from twenty-five years earlier, when war was not a distant abstraction but a minute-by-minute struggle for survival.

At around 10:00, he told Duchamp, he left the VOA studio, took the subway to Christopher Street, and walked along 10th Street toward Matta's apartment. On the way he passed Lam's and noticed that the light was on, so he supposed the artist must still be at home. It was unlike the frugal Lam to leave a light burning when he was out.

Perhaps he had forgotten about the party or was as involved in his work as Breton had been.

He climbed the stoop, intending to ring Lam's bell. Just then someone came out of the building and held the door for him, so he didn't bother to ring. He walked up the three flights and knocked on Lam's door. When he got no response he tried the knob and found the door open. He called out, but there was no answer.

The apartment, one of several in the five-story building, had its entrance door opening into the kitchen. To the right, the large front parlor with a north-facing window served as Lam's studio. To the left, a door led to a small windowless bedroom. The toilet was outside on the landing. Hearing no movement in the studio, Breton had glanced into the bedroom, thinking that Lam might be asleep, but the room was empty. Then he entered the studio and found the artist dead on the floor.

"My God!" exclaimed Duchamp, shaken out of his habitual detachment—like Breton, he seldom lost his composure. "What happened to him?"

"I cannot say," Breton confessed. "There is no evidence of violence, no bleeding or wounds that I could see. I did not examine the body."

"A heart attack, perhaps," suggested Duchamp.

"No, I am certain the cause of death was not natural."

"How do you know?"

"You will see for yourself," Breton told him.

FOUR.

They entered the building without meeting anyone. As they climbed the stairs, Breton advised his companion what to expect.

"You will be as shocked as I was," he warned. "Someone killed him, and whoever it was made the body into a human parody of our Surrealist parlor game."

Duchamp absorbed this news in silence. He had seldom indulged in the game of *cadavre exquis*, a diversion invented by the Surrealists as a means of practicing their trademark creative strategy of "pure psychic automatism." One person would begin a drawing, fold the paper so that the picture was not visible and then pass it to the next person, who would draw another segment, fold the paper again, and pass it on, resulting in an image of mismatched parts that was both absurd and amusing.

Duchamp was not partial to the group activities that the Surrealists used to elicit subconscious imagery for their poems and paintings. They seemed contrived to him, though he had to admit that collective exploits sometimes led to interesting projects, such as the provocative exhibitions he had helped organize in Paris and New York. Chess was his game.

Approaching the apartment, Breton held his friend back a moment.

"Before I open the door," he said, "I must remind you to touch nothing. The police, if they bother to look, will not find my fingerprints, as I am wearing gloves. I hope that whoever did this has left some evidence other than the humiliating costume."

He flipped on the light and directed Duchamp into the studio.

More than the death of a close companion, this loss was sharpened by the knowledge that a Surrealist must be responsible. Who else would think of that collection of disparate elements, attached to the body in such a way as to mimic one of their communal drawings? Each item was familiar, even the giant chicken foot that Lam had found in the trash outside a costume shop and brought back to the studio as a prop for his exotic ritual scenes. The African mask, acquired in the Marché aux Puces, was one of his prized possessions, so much so that he had insisted on taking it with him when they fled Paris. The galosh was one of a pair he wore on rainy days, when the umbrella also served. All these things had been in the apartment, so the killer simply used what was at hand.

But why? It occurred to Duchamp that this was a diversion, done to implicate a Surrealist. Yet only a Surrealist could have thought of it. Only a Surrealist would know what an exquisite corpse looks like—what Lam looked like now.

Breton's experienced eye detected subtle changes. Again he removed his glove and checked the mastoid neck muscle. It was stiffening, indicating death more than three hours earlier.

"We must go to the police station right away," he told Duchamp. "If we delay any longer they will wonder why we waited."

FIVE.

The two friends climbed the steps of the 6th Precinct, on Charles Street, and approached the reception desk. One of them spoke to the desk sergeant in accented English.

"I wish to report a death," he said matter-of-factly, "in an apartment at 140 West 10th Street. It is my friend Wifredo Lam, a painter."

"Name?" said the sergeant.

"Lam, as I said," repeated Duchamp.

"Your name."

"Oh, I beg your pardon. Duchamp. Marcel Duchamp."

"Address?" Duchamp gave it. "210 West 14th Street."

"And who is this with you?"

Breton's name and address were duly given.

At that moment Detective Sergeant John J. O'Connell came on duty, ready for the usual drunk and disorderly traffic, barroom brawls, and occasional knifing, that punctuated every Saturday night in the West Village. The two neatly dressed men at the desk were an unexpected sight. They appeared to be sober, polite and uninjured. He pegged them as victims of a pickpocket.

"What have we here, Sergeant Flynn?" he inquired.

"These French fellas found a pal o' theirs dead in a crib on 10th Street," Flynn replied. "This one don't talk no English." He nodded at Breton. "That one does the talking for 'em both." He gestured at Duchamp.

"Thank you, sergeant. You gentlemen come with me to the interview room. We'll get all the details there."

With Duchamp's help, Breton made his statement, swore to its accuracy and handed over Lam's keys. O'Connell, a doctor, a photographer, and a couple of forensic cops were dispatched to the scene. They searched and dusted the apartment, examined and photographed Lam's remains, called an ambulance, and had the body removed to the morgue. Breton and Duchamp had been kept in the interview room, dozing on hard chairs while the police went about their business. O'Connell wanted them held until he returned.

He had been confused by the description of the body, and he didn't like it. It sounded crazy, and he wanted the witnesses, such as they were, to be around after he had seen this improbable sight for himself. Sure enough, Duchamp had described it accurately.

What he hadn't mentioned was the artistic significance of the costume. If he had, the suspects would all be his friends, and the prospect of implicating them was too daunting. So when Breton blurted out, "Il et arrangé comme un cadavre exquis," Duchamp didn't translate the phrase accurately. He said, "My friend says the corpse is disguised."

Duchamp also didn't—in fact, couldn't—explain why anyone would do that to Lam after he was dead. It certainly wasn't done while he was alive.

You'd have to kill me before I'd let anyone make me look like that, thought O'Connell.

But these are artists, he reminded himself, so who knows what they get up to. Maybe the guy just lay there and let someone decorate him before they did him in. Some stupid game, maybe a sex thing that got out of hand. But except for his shoes and socks Lam was fully clothed, and there were no visible marks on the body. That suggested to O'Connell that he had been smothered. It could have happened while he was lying there being decorated. No, that made no sense, he would have struggled and undone all that perverse handiwork.

There was no evidence of forced entry. The window was locked, but Breton said the apartment door had been open. Lam must have let the killer in, so it was probably someone he knew. They'd all have to be questioned, starting with the friends who were at the party Duchamp mentioned in his statement. Lam was supposed to be there. Maybe one of the other guests stopped by for him, like Breton had done later, and they got into a fight. But there were no signs of violence.

They searched the apartment. Tucked inside Lam's passport was a letter, written in French, postmarked Havana and signed "Je t'embrasse, Helena." That must be the wife Duchamp told them about. Nothing appeared to be missing. The artist had few personal possessions, not surprising for someone who had been uprooted and was on the run for a while. According to Duchamp, he'd been in New York for only about a year and was getting financial help from a rich lady, one of the Guggenheim clan, who ran an art gallery uptown. She would buy a painting outright and try to sell it to pay herself back. Sometimes that worked, but even when it didn't she made sure Lam had rent money. They found $300 in cash in his back pocket, the first place any thief would look. Probably a payment from the Guggenheim dame.

In the studio, Lam's canvases leaned undisturbed against the walls, and a painting in progress, nearly finished, remained on his easel. Like a confused spectator in a silent movie, O'Connell cocked his head and then scratched it, unable to fathom the arcane symbolism in the abstraction of stylized figures, some brandishing what looked like weapons, in a tropical jungle. The officer who had been dusting for fingerprints asked what he made of it, and the detective replied that he was damned if he knew.

"Looks like the natives are restless," observed the officer drily.

"Looks like they're downright murderous," O'Connell replied. "Maybe they did it."

Although there was no way to know whether any sketches or drawings had been taken, it didn't seem likely. Maybe the African mask was worth something to a collector, but that was still there, covering Lam's face. And the cash was still there, too. If robbery wasn't the motive, what was? And what possible reason would someone have for the bizarre post-mortem get-up?

These enigmas were complicated by the fact that Lam was half Afro-Cuban and half Chinese, two cultures as mysterious to O'Connell as the circumstances of the artist's death. Both had footholds in New York, the Chinese nearby on and around Canal Street, the Cubans in a smaller enclave uptown in Spanish Harlem. Apart from his Parisian expatriate circle, Lam might have a connection to either or both communities.

Unfortunately for O'Connell, this not only widened the investigation's scope but also took it into unknown territory.

Sunday morning, October 17

SIX.

The sun had been up for nearly half an hour when Breton and Duchamp were finally released. After a virtually sleepless night in the interrogation room, drinking bad coffee and eating stale donuts, they were more than ready to part ways. When they reached Greenwich Street, Breton thanked his friend for sharing his ordeal and turned north toward his apartment. Although he wanted nothing more than sleep, good manners dictated an invitation. "Will you come in for coffee—real coffee, that is?" he inquired.

"No, I think not, thank you," replied Duchamp politely. "I must tell Peggy what has happened, and I must do it in person."

The subway took Duchamp north to East 59th Street, two blocks from Peggy Guggenheim's town house. By the time he reached her door, exhaustion was catching up with him. It was only 8:00 a.m., and Peggy never rose before 10:00 on Sundays, but the maid let him in, took his overcoat, settled him in the parlor, and went to awaken her mistress.

His disheveled appearance stopped Peggy as she entered the room, still wearing her negligee. He was normally so fastidious, so nicely turned out. Even if his well-tailored clothes showed their age, they were always clean and pressed. This morning they were rumpled, and he needed a shave.

"My dear Luigi," she began, addressing him by his pet name, "you look all in. Something is wrong, I know it."

His weary eyes found hers. It was hard for him to focus. His words came in short bursts.

"It's Lam. He's dead. Murdered, it seems. Breton found him. We've been with the police all night. I had to translate."

Peggy dropped beside him on the sofa, her face flushed with astonishment. "Who on earth would do such a thing? Where was he?"

Duchamp began to describe the circumstances, but he faltered. "Dear Peggy, may I rest awhile? I can hardly keep my head up. I will tell you all I know after I've had some sleep."

Stifling her curiosity, Peggy led him to her bedroom, helped him off with his jacket, and offered him a pair of silk pajamas she had bought for her husband, Max Ernst, who had never worn them—not because he didn't sleep in pajamas, but because he seldom slept in the town house. He and Peggy were not on the best of terms.

"I'll leave you now," she said. "I won't disturb you. Tell me everything when you awaken. But one thing I must know before you sleep. Where did it happen? Oh yes, and where did you report it?"

"His apartment," Duchamp mumbled, "and we went to the local precinct. A few blocks away. On Charles Street."

He slumped in a chair and began to remove his trousers as Peggy discreetly left the room. He was nearly asleep when he climbed into the bed, still warm from her body, and quickly drifted into unconsciousness.

Back in the parlor, Peggy was consulting her address book. As the niece of wealthy, prominent New York businessmen, she moved in a social circle far wider

21

than the tight-knit art world that included both the European émigrés and the American avant-garde whose work she showed in her 57th Street gallery, Art of This Century. While they lived and worked downtown, she was cultivating an uptown clientele. Her gallery receptions attracted a cosmopolitan crowd, many of whom were family friends. Among them was Lewis Valentine, the Police Commissioner, whose home telephone number she found and dialed.

When Theresa Valentine answered the phone, Peggy asked if her husband were at home. "I hope I'm not disturbing your Sunday breakfast," she said.

"Oh, no, not at all," replied Mrs. Valentine graciously. "Lewis and I are just back from Mass, and we had a light breakfast before we went. He's right here, Peggy. I'll put him on."

Valentine came to the phone expecting a summons to one of Peggy's soirées, or perhaps to a charity function for the war effort. Her gallery had opened a year ago, and its first event had been a benefit reception for the American Red Cross.

"I apologize for calling you at home," Peggy began, "but I wanted you to be aware of a case in which I have a personal interest. One of my artists, Wifredo Lam—the dark-skinned Cuban fellow, I believe you and Theresa met him at my party in March—has been murdered. He was found dead in his apartment on West 10th Street in Greenwich Village. I understand that the local precinct is investigating the crime, and I should be deeply grateful if you would make sure it's properly handled."

After ten years in office and with hundreds of murder investigations behind him, Valentine wasted no time on commiserations.

"Why of course, my dear Peggy. Please spell his name for me. That'll be the 6th Precinct's jurisdiction. When was the body found? Late last night, you say. Well,

22

they won't have the autopsy report yet, but I'm sure the detective in charge—probably O'Connell, if I remember rightly—has already begun his inquiries. He's a top man, he'll solve it, don't you worry. We can't have people killing off your artists, now can we?"

He regretted that flip remark as soon as the words were spoken.

"Please forgive me, Peggy, that was patronizing. I shouldn't have implied that this case is anything less than serious. I've been in this job too long, I guess. You get pretty hardened to tragedy when you deal with it every day."

Peggy rescued him before he could dig himself in any deeper. "I understand completely, Lewis. I know I can rely on you to do whatever you can to bring whoever is responsible to justice."

She replaced the receiver with a feeling of satisfaction. Far from taking offense at Valentine's faux pas, she sensed that it would make him all the more determined to ensure that the investigation would be thorough and the killer found. She smiled to herself as she returned to her bedroom, where Duchamp lay deep asleep.

Shrugging off her negligee, she climbed naked between the sheets and nestled against him, feeling the contours of his lean body under the smooth silk. Gently, so as not to disturb him, she slipped a hand inside the pajama trousers. When he awoke, she would help him forget for a time the sad circumstances of his visit to her bed.

SEVEN.

O'Connell's shift had officially ended more than an hour ago, but he wanted to make one stop before heading home to Brooklyn. He had already ordered the beat cop to talk to Lam's neighbors and assigned Detective Patrick Collins to interview the host of last night's party, after which he was to take the subway uptown to East Harlem and inquire about Lam's possible ties to the Cuban immigrant community.

That left the Chinatown connection to investigate, and O'Connell knew better than to send one of his officers nosing around in that neighborhood. All doors would be closed to a Caucasian cop working outside his jurisdiction. He had to take a roundabout route, and fortunately he had one, via someone he'd encountered in the station house a few times—an artist with an unfortunate tendency to land in the tank overnight. He opened a file drawer, pulled out a nearly full pint bottle of Four Roses, slipped it into his overcoat pocket and set off.

A short walk to Seventh Avenue led him to a rundown loft building with dirty windows and a battered doorway where derelicts could often be found huddled in the recess. This morning it was vacant, and O'Connell rang the second-floor bell. He could hear the chime faintly, but had to give it a few more hits before he got a response.

24

Finally the buzzer released the latch and he entered the tiled hallway, rank with the odor of unemptied garbage pails and oily paint rags. He climbed to the second floor and knocked.

"Come in," a voice croaked. "I left it open."

Yun Gee's studio was a certified mess. It was apparent to O'Connell that Gee's wife Helen hadn't been here in a while, maybe never, and also that Gee hadn't gone home to their apartment for several days. Could be they're having marital troubles, he speculated, and the guy decided to lay low for a while. Sure looks like he's been drowning his sorrows.

In addition to the clutter one would expect in an artist's studio, there were dirty dishes, a pile of clothes and bedding, and a couple of empty liquor bottles littering the floor around Gee, who was seated on a sagging couch that apparently doubled as a bed. The only other furniture, apart from a sturdy easel and a long worktable improvised from plywood and sawhorses, was a three-legged stool and a discarded office chair rescued from the street. O'Connell rolled the chair over to Gee, who showed no inclination to rise and greet his guest.

The detective pulled out the whiskey bottle, retrieved a grimy glass from the litter, wiped it with his handkerchief, poured a stiff shot, and handed it to the artist.

"Hair of the dog," he advised. "Your health."

The irony was not lost on Gee, who grinned and sipped the drink gingerly. "Early in the day for me, but thanks."

"I'm the one to be thanking you," said O'Connell, "because you're going to help me out. You know all the artists around here. You know one who's half Chinese, name of Lam?"

Gee's grin widened into a smile. "A Chinaman? Also an artist? Of course I know Lam. He's not really Chinese, in spite of his name. He's really Cuban. His dad

25

went there from Hong Kong to work the sugar, married a Negro girl." Gee's own father had followed a similar path, coming to the United States from Kwangtung as a laborer. Settled in San Francisco in 1921, he sent for his fifteen-year-old son. Like Lam, the young aspiring artist gravitated to Paris, and then to New York, then back to Paris.

"Like all of us,' Gee continued, "he wanted to be modern. He went to art school in Spain, but it was too traditional for him. He got a good reception in Paris. An important Spanish guy, Picasso, looked after him, helped him plenty. But the Nazis kicked him out, his friends too, and they all came to New York. I was here already, got out in '39."

Gee took another sip of whiskey. Another smile, rueful this time, more to himself than to O'Connell. "So we met up again. Like old home week."

O'Connell doubted that an artist's life in wartime New York was anything like the pre-war Parisian scene, which he imagined as glamorous in a gritty, bohemian way, certainly a lot more stimulating than the materialistic American culture they were stuck in now. At least they were alive. It would be a different story if they'd fallen into Hitler's hands. But he didn't want Gee to turn nostalgic, so he let the remark hang.

"When you and Lam got together," he asked, "did you spend much time in Chinatown? Does he have any connections there?"

Gee shook his head and took another sip. "Don't think so," he replied. "I go a lot, to get special tea and herbs. We ate there a couple of times. I wanted to show him real Chinese food, but he likes Cuban better. Mostly he cooks for himself, but he eats out at a Cuban restaurant when he sells a picture. He took me once. Here in the West Village."

"Little Havana, on Cornelia Street?"

Another sip. "Yes, I think that's it."

O'Connell put the bottle on the floor, where the artist could reach it easily, and got down to business. "Yun, I'd like you to do me a favor," he began. "The reason I'm asking about Lam is because he was killed last night, and I want to find out who did it. Will you help me?"

Gee almost dropped his glass. He stared at the detective, clearly horrified. "What? He's dead? How?"

"We don't know much yet. I have to wait for the autopsy to find out the cause of death, but he was killed in his apartment, probably in the early evening. A friend found his body around 10:30 p.m., and he hadn't been dead long."

O'Connell didn't mention the decorations. Gee was upset enough, no need to make it any more gruesome. "The favor is this," he explained. "Will you ask around, quiet like, in Chinatown? Find out if any of the tong boys know him. It's just a hunch of mine, but I can't shake the feeling it ought to be followed up on."

He tried to make it sound like a casual request, but they both knew it could be dangerous. You messed with the tongs at your peril. They peddled information to the police when it suited their purposes, but they dealt harshly with unauthorized snitches. Gee would have to be very careful how he handled it.

With an unsteady hand, the artist reached down for the bottle. He refilled his glass and took a long swallow of liquid courage. "I'll ask and let you know," he promised.

EIGHT.

Breton opened his apartment door to the sound of his daughter Aube singing along with the gramophone in the front parlor, as she watched her mother practicing on the trapeze.

Jacqueline Lamba's lithe body wrapped itself around the crossbar and uncoiled into a swan dive pose, perfectly balanced on the horizontal support. Her skin-tight leotard showed off the athletic figure that had captivated audiences at the Café du Dôme, where she had performed underwater acrobatics in a giant fish tank. Breton had been among the most deeply captivated. Their passionate affair and subsequent marriage inspired several of his poems, but Lamba's ardor had begun to cool when Breton's fellow Surrealists failed to take her seriously as an artist.

They were notorious for objectifying their women, and their misogyny was only enhanced by Lamba's beauty. They had included a few of her watercolors and collages in their exhibitions, but she knew it was only because she was Breton's wife. In Paris she relied on him for entrée into the stimulating creative and intellectual milieu that was revolutionizing art and literature, yet she could never become a full-fledged member in her own right. She was growing more independent in New York, where she was no longer constrained by their tight-knit circle.

If she and Aube heard Breton enter, they did not acknowledge his presence. Aube continued to sing, and Lamba went on with her practice routine. After his ordeal at the precinct and the five-flight climb to their apartment, he was too tired to interrupt, and anyway he dreaded telling her what had happened. He had been out all night, and that would have to be explained as well. Instead he made his way to the bedroom and barely got his overcoat off before falling onto the bed, enormously grateful for its softness. He managed to kick off his shoes and loosen his tie before sleep overtook him.

Half an hour later, her routine finished, Lamba bathed and dressed quickly. She kissed Aube on each cheek, told her not to wake her father, and left the apartment. The seven-year-old girl was quiet and studious, perfectly content to read or draw or play by herself all day. She spoke hardly any English, so she had no friends her own age outside the Lycée Français de New York, for which their American benefactor, David Hare, was paying.

Lamba had learned English at school, which gave her a distinct advantage in her new surroundings. That morning she had an appointment. She descended quickly to the first floor, let herself out of the building, ran down the stoop, then headed east, to 42 Bleecker Street.

NINE.

Matta's apartment was at 5 Patchin Place, in the row of 19th century buildings lining the picturesque cul-de-sac's east side. Collins rang the bell at 9:00 a.m., by which hour, he thought, all decent Christians should be awake, especially on a Sunday. He had been to early Mass and ridden the subway in from Queens to take the morning shift, so his day was well along.

It took several rings to get a response. Two flights up, he was admitted to a room that was in shambles from the previous night's revels. Overflowing ashtrays, half-empty glasses of wine and liquor, soggy crackers topped with curling cheese slices. A man asleep on the couch filled out the décor. Matta was unshaven and obviously hung over. He eyed the detective with apprehension when Collins identified himself and displayed his shield.

"Was there a complaint about the party?" he asked. His English, enriched by the lilt of his native Spanish, was excellent. "I thought the downstairs neighbors were away this weekend."

"No complaint, sir," answered Collins. "I'm here on another matter." As he spoke, he realized that the last word, pronounced with his New York accent, sounded just like this fellow's surname, and he looked momentarily embarrassed.

In spite of the artist's condition, his well-known wit had not deserted him. "One Matta is all you will get today, officer. My wife and kids are out of town."

"Let's go into my studio," he suggested. "We don't want to disturb the sleeping beauty."

He led the way to what had been the front parlor, which now housed his workspace. In addition to the usual tools and materials, a painting in progress on an easel, and a shelf full of art books and catalogues, the room boasted a pair of upholstered chairs, shabby but comfortable, and an electric hot plate.

Matta directed Collins to one of the chairs and asked if he wanted coffee or tea, which the detective declined. The artist's manner was relaxed, perhaps a bit too casual in light of the fact that he didn't yet know the purpose of the inquiry. He's not firing on all cylinders, thought Collins, but that's about to change.

"Last night," he began, "you had a number of guests, your artist friends, I'm told." He didn't stop to explain how he knew this. "One of them, a fellow called Breton, came in late and left quickly with his pal Duchamp." Collins's pronunciation contorted the names, but Matta knew whom he meant. "Do you know why they went off so suddenly?"

Matta shrugged. "Frankly, officer, I didn't see Breton arrive and I don't know when Duchamp left. It must have been while I was here in the studio, discussing my latest painting with a colleague. When we came out Duchamp was gone, but I didn't think anything of it."

Suddenly it dawned on Matta that Collins had information about his own party that even he wasn't aware of. He became guarded.

"How do you know who came and went from here? And why are you asking me about them?"

Now Collins had to decide how much to reveal. He was trained to withhold as much information as possible

31

and, when required to answer a question, to be as vague as possible. The reasoning was that suspects were more likely to give something away if they didn't know where the questioning was leading.

But Matta wasn't really a suspect, though the time of death hadn't yet been firmly established. If Lam were killed in the early evening, Matta probably would have been able to do the deed and get back to his apartment in plenty of time to greet his first guests. Could be he had a grudge against the guy, some personal score to settle. Collins decided to see how he would react to the news of Lam's death.

"I'm inquiring into an incident that was reported by Breton and Duchamp last night," he began, choosing his words carefully. "According to the report, Breton called on a fellow named Wifredo Lam, who was supposed to be here at your party, and found him dead on the floor."

Matta was suddenly alert. His guarded expression dissolved into what Collins took to be the astonishment you'd naturally feel when told of a close friend's sudden death. But it was alarm that caused Matta's head to jerk back, his brows to knit, and his mouth to open with a quick intake of breath. He stared at Collins in what appeared to be utter confusion, a mixture of shock and disbelief. He doesn't know how to react, his hangover is in the way, was Collins's assessment. That was true, but it wasn't the cause of Matta's anxiety. His worries went deeper.

Then his Spanish fatalism kicked in, and it dawned on him that nature must have played a cruel trick on Lam, as well as himself. His expression softened and turned inward. He sighed heavily.

"Poor Lam," he muttered. "He's been through so much. Uprooted, hiding out, never knowing if the next knock on the door would be the Gestapo. We were all in danger, but he more than the rest because of his color. Before the war it was easier for him in Paris than New

York, as you may imagine. Until Hitler and his racial purists arrived."

He shook his head, silently indicting the prejudice he perceived as endemic to American culture, and which was even more sinister in Nazi ideology.

"Was it his heart?"

Either he's a great actor, Collins thought, or he really doesn't know that Lam was murdered.

"No, sir," he answered. "It was not from natural causes."

"Then what happened? An accident?"

"Apparently not, though the actual cause hasn't yet been determined. It appears someone killed him."

Matta was speechless. His expression changed again, this time to wide-eyed amazement. He stared at Collins as if seeing him for the first time. When he did speak, it was almost a whisper, in his native tongue.

"Madre de Dios."

TEN.

After taking down the names and addresses of as many of Lam's friends as Matta could recall—his memory was not helped by his morning-after state or his distress—Collins decided to hang around Patchin Place instead of returning to the station. He had a hunch that Matta would need to share the news with someone, and he wanted to find out who that might be. His experienced scan of the apartment confirmed that there was no telephone, so it would have to be done in person, or from a public pay phone. He crossed 10th Street to the police box on the corner and rang the precinct. Sergeant Joseph Ryan was on desk duty.

"Joe, it's Pat here. I've just come from interviewing that artist guy who threw the party last night. I want to keep an eye on him for a bit, no special reason. He's up in the apartment now, but if he comes down I'm gonna follow him, just in case he leads me somewhere interesting. Don't know how long I'll be, so you'd better send someone else up to Harlem to check out the Cubans."

The sergeant was hesitant. "We got Fitzgerald, but he don't speak Spanish."

"Don't need to," Collins told him. "He's to go straight to the 23rd. Call ahead and get Officer Diaz to meet him. She knows the territory and everybody in it."

"She?" said Ryan, certain he had misheard.

"That's right, boyo. Juanita Diaz. She's tough, smart, and a good one to have at your back in that neighborhood. I worked with her on a weapons case a year or so ago, and I would've been lost without her. Tell Fitz to be respectful. She's a bit sensitive."

"Don't worry, Pat. Fitz'll handle it okay."

"Have the photos come in yet? He'll need some ID shots."

"A courier brought 'em over from the morgue about ten minutes ago," Ryan told him. "I'll see to it that he gets as many as he needs."

Just then Matta emerged from his building and walked down the alley, past the iron gate that barred the drive, and onto 10th Street. Collins turned away, told Ryan he was moving and rang off. The artist went left, then downtown on Sixth Avenue. He turned onto Bleecker Street and headed east. Collins followed at a good distance, though his quarry seemed to be paying no attention to anyone or anything around him. There was hardly any motor traffic on a Sunday morning, but Matta managed to step in front of the solitary taxi cruising Broadway.

Good thing for him the cabbie's a lot more alert than he is, thought Collins. He's got plenty on his mind. Is it just sorrow he's feeling? Maybe he and Lam were really close. But he couldn't dismiss the notion that there was something more behind Matta's agitation, and his rush to head out suggested it was worthwhile to follow that instinct.

It was turning into a fine October day, Lord be praised. Collins hated tailing people in the rain.

ELEVEN.

Endowed with a head of ginger hair, emerald eyes, and a dusting of freckles on his cheeks, Officer Brian F.X. Fitzgerald was the epitome of the Irish cop. Not that he stood out in a department long dominated by immigrants from Ireland and their descendants. True to form, he was following in the footsteps of his father, and of his father's father, and of his father before him. Brought to this country as an infant during the Great Hunger, Fitzgerald's great-grandfather had joined the force in 1873, when it was already half Irish.

Brian's mother would have preferred the security and safety of the priesthood for her first-born, but his hero-worship of his father—as well as his robust attraction to the opposite sex—set him on a different path. He did well in high school, breezed through the Police Academy entrance exam, and joined the force at twenty. Now, still a bachelor six years later, he was thinking of settling down.

The only catch was finding the right girl. Everyone had expected him to tie the knot with Mary Dolan, his high school sweetheart. But they'd been drifting for some time, and had broken up a year ago. There was no denying he cared for her—he'd told her that often enough—but something kept holding him back. We know each other too well, he rationalized to himself, we're more like brother and sister. Then he would see-saw, review her many assets, and conclude that she was just right for him. Still, he couldn't bring himself to pop the question.

Sick of their on-again, off-again romance, Mary enlisted in the WAVES in fall 1942 and shipped out to the Naval Air Station in Kansas, where she promptly snagged herself a dashing flyboy.

"Such a lovely girl. You're a fool to let her slip," his mother had scolded, while his father winked a knowing eye and confided that there were plenty of other pebbles on the beach. Especially with so many eligible young men overseas.

TWELVE.

Carrying several headshots and a full portrait of Lam's body in costume, Fitzgerald headed uptown to the 23rd Precinct. Ryan had called to alert Officer Diaz, who would serve as his liaison to the Spanish-speaking community and specifically the Cuban contingent.

She was waiting at the desk when Fitz arrived. He had tried to form a mental picture of her as he rode north on the subway and had come up with the image of a matronly type of no-nonsense female cop, with sallow skin, black hair pulled back in a practical bun, and a thick Spanish accent. His stereotyping left him unprepared for the tall redhead who greeted him. He was five foot nine, and her eyes were level with his. Her hair fell to her shoulders in auburn waves.

One look told her that her fellow cop had expected someone very different.

"Officer Fitzgerald, a pleasure," she greeted him politely, her English accented by the slurred consonants of a New York City native. Her handshake was firm but not aggressive. She held it for a few moments to give him time to recover while she chatted amiably.

"I look forward to working with you. From what your sergeant told me, it's an interesting case. He didn't give me much detail, but I'm sure you'll fill me in."

Fitzgerald's double take had settled into a cross between confusion and pleasant surprise. The extended handshake had also given him time to find his voice, although not his full composure.

"Yes, ma'am, I sure will. I mean, yes. Officer Diaz."

Her smile was alarmingly genial. "Please call me Nita."

"I answer to Fitz."

"I think we'll get along fine, Fitz. Downtown cops don't come this far north very often, but I worked a case with a detective from the 6th not too long ago. Collins is his name."

Fitz was starting to relax. "We're both on this one," he said. "It's a killing, maybe manslaughter, maybe homicide. I guess Ryan told you that the victim is Cuban. I want to find out if he was involved in anything up here that could have got him killed."

Nita nodded. "Let's go back to the office and you can give me the details." She paused and came to a decision.

"I know you're wondering about me," she said as they walked down the hall. "My family is Cuban, too. They were bankers down in Havana. My parents came to New York before I was born. My dad opened a branch of the bank here in Harlem. Hispanics were just beginning to displace the Italians in this neighborhood, and he thought the community was underserved. He was right. None of the Anglo banks wanted to do business with the immigrants.

"Dad's bank was there for folks who'd never had savings or checking accounts before, or access to loans so they could buy furniture or open a business. When the Depression hit, and a lot of his customers lost their jobs or their earnings fell off, he carried their loans. It was a financial lifeline for many families around here.

"One day, when I was eighteen, an armed robber entered the bank. My father confronted him, and the robber shot him dead. The guy ran out and was never caught. The police investigation was pathetic. They dragged it out until it was too late. Word on the street was that the Cosa Nostra paid them off and shipped the guy back to Italy." She shook her head ruefully.

"It devastated our family, we had to sell the bank. I told my mother I wanted to become a police officer so I could work from the inside and find out who was responsible. She thought I was crazy. 'Let your brother do it,' she said, but I knew the force wasn't for him. He was such a sweet kid, never got into trouble. He wanted to be a musician."

Her brow furrowed. "So where is he now? Fighting for his life on some godforsaken island in the Pacific. And here I am, wearing a different uniform and fighting my own battles on the home front. I still want to find out who killed my father, even if it's true that he's out of reach. That's why I'm a cop."

Her frankness impressed him. "That's as good a reason as I've ever heard," he said, "but I don't suppose you get much time to investigate such a cold case."

"No, it's more a matter of keeping my ear to the ground, hoping something or someone will lead me in the right direction. After five years on the force I've got a reputation as the precinct's chief snoop."

They had reached the office, and Fitz held the door for her. "No wonder Collins put me onto you," he said aloud, and to himself, I'm sure glad he did.

As they entered, Nita tossed her head and looked back at him, anticipating his unspoken question. "Yes, it's natural. I come from a long line of fire-breathing redheads."

Fitz removed his cap and ran his hand over his own carrot top. "You could be talking about my family, too."

40

"If my dad had been a bit less like that he might still be alive. But solving that killing will have to wait a bit longer."

She directed him to a regulation hard wooden chair, and took one for herself. "Let's go over your case. What have you got?"

"Not much," Fitz told her. He pushed a headshot across the desk. "He was an artist, half Cuban Negro, half Chinese."

"Now there's a combination." She studied the picture thoughtfully. "Any reason to believe that either community is involved?"

"Apparently he let the killer in, so it was someone he knew, or wasn't wary of. He had to open two doors for him."

"Or her," Nita added.

"Right you are. Can't rule out anything at this early stage. We don't have the medical examiner's report yet, so even the cause of death is unknown."

"No marks, no wounds?"

"No evident ones, according to O'Connell's crime scene report. He was the detective on duty when the guys who found the body came in."

Fitz hesitated, not wanting to offend Nita. He was already feeling a mixture of respect and attraction. "One peculiar thing. The body had a weird costume on."

He pulled out the crime scene photograph. Nita studied it with interest.

"The report says it was put on him after death, he didn't do the getup himself. His friends, the ones who found him, said they had no idea why he was dressed up like that. But the guys at the station, uh, they have an idea. They think it's a Cuban voodoo thing, especially since he's part Negro. I'm sure not everybody from the islands does that pagan stuff, but I have to check it out. Is there anything like that going on up here?"

41

"I know what Anglos think of us," she said, then corrected herself. "Some of them, anyway. I don't want to generalize either." She smiled reassuringly. "In fact, there are a few older folks who practice Santería—that's the Cuban version of voodoo—but it's not big here. I know a self-styled priestess, really more of a fortune-teller and traditional healer. She can probably tell you if there's anything to link this costume to Santería ritual."

Fitz gathered up the photographs. "Okay, let's go see her."

THIRTEEN.

A half-mile walk down Varick Street and across Canal took Yun Gee into the heart of Chinatown. Heading east, he took a right on Mott, then turned into a narrow alley beside a nondescript restaurant, its filthy windows, peeling paint, and lack of English-language signs calculated to repel tourists.

A man dressed as a cook lounged by the rear door. In reality he was a sentry guarding the entrance to the headquarters of the On Leong Association, Chinatown's most powerful tong. As soon as he saw Gee, he straightened and reached a hand under his apron, where a knife was sheathed on his belt.

Gee approached slowly, keeping both hands visible. He addressed the sentry in Cantonese. "I am Yun Gee. I wish to pay my respects, and to petition your master, whose shoes I am unworthy to kiss."

The sentry's cold eyes appraised him. "Wait here." He unlocked the back door and disappeared into the hall, locking the door behind him.

Presently the door opened and the sentry beckoned Gee inside, where a large bodyguard was waiting to escort him. The man was well over six feet tall, and massively built. Bulging muscles strained his suit jacket. A shoulder holster distorted it even more.

43

After a thorough frisking. Gee was shown to an unmarked door halfway down the hall. The bodyguard knocked lightly, opened the door and led him inside, then closed the door and stationed himself in front of it. Not a word had been spoken since Gee entered the building.

The windowless room was strictly utilitarian. A small shaded lamp on an elaborately carved wooden desk that showed years of rough use was the only light. Packing crates labeled in Chinese characters were stacked along one wall. A single restaurant chair stood well back from the desk. Behind the desk sat a slender figure in a silk robe.

A hand on Gee's back directed him to the chair and another on his shoulder compelled him to sit. From that vantage he could see the figure's arms resting on the desk, with its hands tucked Hollywood-cliché-style into richly embroidered sleeves. The massive desk blocked all but the upper body, and the shaded light left the face largely obscured, but Gee knew he was sitting opposite the man who controlled most of Chinatown's commerce, both legitimate and illegal.

There was no need for Gee to introduce himself. The tongs had a line on New York's entire Chinese community, especially those who lived in and around Chinatown. He waited until he was spoken to.

"Your visit honors me." The voice was soft, slightly high-pitched, almost feminine. "How may I be of service?"

Gee had given much thought to his approach. Indirection, he decided, was imperative.

"I come in sorrow," he began. "I mourn the loss of a dear friend, a fellow artist, Wifredo Lam."

"The name is known to me. What happened to him?"

Aware of the superstition against speaking of death directly, Gee obfuscated. "He joined his ancestors last night, before his time. An intruder, apparently."

"But not identified." It was a statement, not a question. "I see. You wish revenge."

"No, not revenge," Gee replied, even though that would have been appropriate by tong standards. "I would like justice."

Yun thought he detected a smile on the shadowed face.

"You are becoming American. It is your wife's influence, no doubt. A fine woman, you are fortunate. She has given you a beautiful daughter."

A shiver ran up Gee's back. It was not an overt threat, but a reminder that he and his family were vulnerable. The police would be powerless to prevent retribution if he ran afoul of On Leong.

He hoped his face didn't betray his apprehension. To cover it he broke into a broad grin.

"Yes, my little Li-Lan is beautiful indeed, and very clever. I am teaching her our language."

"Let us hope she will grow to honor her father and her ancestors." The soft voice hardened slightly. "Meanwhile we must turn our attention to the intruder. I will have inquiries made."

The hand returned to Gee's shoulder, indicating that the audience was over. He had to suppress a sigh of relief. So much had remained unsaid. He hadn't given Lam's address, or the time of death, or the circumstances. Such details were unnecessary. It was assumed that Gee was looking for Lam's killer in the Chinese community, that law enforcement would take over once a suspect was identified, and if that led them to the tong, he would face personal consequences.

Frankly, he thought, if the killer did turn out to be Chinese, straightforward revenge, courtesy of On Leong, would mean a lot less trouble for him. He stood and bowed deeply.

"I am humbled by your concern. Lam was a great artist, a credit to his people. We must know if one of us has wronged him."

"We will know. You will be informed."

FOURTEEN.

A sign in the front window of the ground-floor apartment on East 110th Street identified Madame Carmen as a spiritual advisor and announced that she was open for business. The sign sported a staring eye on the left and a circle with three dots on the right. Nita explained the significance.

"She's playing to two audiences—the ordinary ones who want their fortunes told, and the Santería believers. That symbol on the right is *otanes*, the stones that represent their deities."

As they entered the vestibule, a bell sounded inside the apartment. The door to the front parlor was open, so they stepped in.

Madame Carmen's consulting room was sparsely furnished. Dark drapes covered the windows, and a few chairs were placed against the walls. There was a fireplace with plastic flowers in the grate and candles on the mantle. In the center, a circular table covered in red velvet cloth was set with a crystal ball and a deck of Tarot cards. A tall oak armchair sat behind it, also decorated in red velvet. Two heavily shaded floor lamps glowed dimly on either side of a black-curtained door at the back. A whiff of incense hung in the air.

The curtains parted, and Madame Carmen stepped into the room. Here was the Latina stereotype Fitz had envisioned, but outfitted in gypsy costume instead of a police uniform. Like a character in a music-hall revue, she wore giant hoop earrings, a checkered headscarf from which a tangle of artificially black curls struggled to emerge, and a bright green tasseled shawl over an electric blue satin dress that emphasized her ample proportions.

"Buenos dias, Juanita. Your visit is always a delight. You bring another handsome Anglo policeman. How many do you have on the string?" she teased in Spanish.

"Only one at a time, Madame. I wear one out, and then they send another. But let's speak English."

"Of course, how impolite of me. I apologize. Welcome, officer." She waved her guests to chairs, but Fitz demurred.

"Thank you kindly, Madame Carmen, but this isn't a social call. We want to ask your advice about a case we're working on. It involves a Cuban national." He pulled out a headshot of Lam and handed it to her. "Have you ever seen this man?"

No sooner had she taken the photo from him than she dropped it on the table and pulled her hand back as if she'd touched hot metal.

"Muerto," she whispered. "That man is dead."

Maybe there's something to this clairvoyance thing, Fitz thought. A good look would tell anybody that it's a photo of a corpse, but the light in here's too low for her to have seen it clearly.

"You're right," he told her. "Let's go over to the window and crack the drapes so you can see his face. I'll hold the picture for you."

Reluctantly she followed him to the front of the room. He pulled back the curtain and held the photograph up to the light. She studied it carefully.

"I do not know him. He is of mixed blood, I see. Tell me about him."

Fitz explained what was known so far and then got to the point. This time he prepared her. "What I'm going to show you is the crime scene photo," he explained. "Whoever killed him dressed up the body in a very strange way. I want to know if you can tell me whether it has anything to do with Santería." The light from the window showed the details clearly.

Madame Carmen shook her head vehemently. "In Santería this would be blasphemous! We do not defile our dead with umbrellas and chicken's feet." She turned away in disgust.

"It could be a clumsy attempt to implicate a Santería follower," suggested Nita, "or a deliberate act of disrespect."

Madame looked skeptical. "But why was he killed? If you know the reason, you will find the killer, and he will tell you why he put those things on the body."

"There is no clear motive," Fitz explained. "At this point, we don't even know how he died, much less who killed him. As I told you, robbery doesn't seem likely. Nothing is missing as far as we can tell. He was an artist, living alone, pretty much from hand to mouth."

"Alone, you say?" Madame asked. She reached out and took the crime scene photo, laid it flat on the table, and covered it with her hands.

"Where is his wife?" she asked.

Again Fitz wondered whether she might actually have some kind of second sight. How could she know Lam was married? But he was trained not to show his surprise. "According to his friends, his wife is with his family in Cuba."

"I feel a woman's aura," she continued. "Perhaps a lover in the wife's absence? There is anger in the room, whether his or hers I cannot tell." She moved her hands slowly over the photograph.

"Something else, too. Fear. It leaves a bad feeling, very strong."

FIFTEEN.

It was fear that motivated Matta as he hurried across Lafayette Street and up to the door of the loft building at 42 Bleecker. Following not too far behind him, Collins crossed the street and positioned himself in the stairwell of the subway station opposite.

The curtains on the first-floor window were drawn. Matta leaned over and rapped on the glass several times.

"David" he cried. "It's Matta. Let me in. I must talk to you."

David Hare lifted his head from between Jacqueline Lamba's legs. "Not now. Come back later." he shouted.

"This can't wait." Matta insisted. He hit the window again, hard enough to rattle the aging frame.

"All right, all right, stop that racket," replied Hare angrily. "Meet me in the coffee shop on the corner. I'll be there in a few minutes."

From across the street, Collins couldn't make out what Hare said. He watched Matta leave Hare's door and turn toward Lafayette. The street was nearly deserted. Gas rationing kept automobile traffic to an essential minimum even during the week, and on a Sunday morning it was virtually nonexistent.

Collins hung back as long as he could and was preparing to follow when Matta went into the coffee shop.

From the stairwell Collins could keep the entrance in sight without being visible from the window. In that position he could also keep an eye on Hare's building. The artist's name and address were on the list of Lam's friends that Matta had given him. It wasn't long before he saw a tall, rail-thin young man, his bushy flaxen hair disheveled and his expression grumpy, come out of the loft and head for the coffee shop. That must be Hare, thought Collins. An appropriate name, given that mop on his head. Why did he want to meet outside instead of at his place, he wondered.

Hare slid into the booth opposite Matta. He was not glad to see his friend. A waitress approached and took their order for two coffees.

"Damn you, what's so urgent? You interrupted something important."

"I know what I interrupted," Matta replied. "You and Jacqueline don't exactly keep your affair a secret. I can't understand why Breton puts up with it."

Hare let out a snort. "Yes you can. Breton needs me to publish his journal and pay for his kid's school. Fucking his wife is a small compensation for those services."

Hare's family fortune allowed him to indulge his enthusiasms, and in return his involvement with the Surrealists had substantial professional benefits. It gave credibility to his fledgling artistic career, which had begun modestly a few years earlier with experiments in manipulated photography and could easily have been dismissed as a dilettante's dabbling.

Fortunately for him, his cousin, the Surrealist painter Kay Sage—another of the American expatriates who had returned from Europe—introduced him to the European artists in her circle, and he had felt an immediate kinship with their iconoclastic attitudes. Even though he couldn't speak their language, he appreciated their aims and quickly attached himself to their coattails.

52

His attraction to Lamba was magnetic from the start, and they used her English fluency as an excuse for their relationship. With her as his go-between, he underwrote Breton's magazine, *VVV*, and became an invaluable liaison with the New York intelligentsia.

That mutual dependence accounted for his cynicism, which gave way to a more nuanced explanation.

"Besides, Breton has nothing to say about it. Jacqueline and I are in love. She's going to leave him and marry me."

"Let's forget your sex life," Matta snapped. "You won't be in the mood when I tell you the news. Lam is dead, killed in his apartment. The police came around this morning wanting to know who his friends are. They think one of us did it."

Hare stiffened, his amazement evident on his face. "Jesus Christ. When did it happen?"

"Last night."

"But we were all at your place."

"It was earlier, they think. Before the party. Breton found him at around 10:30, then headed for my place. Did you see him come in? I was in the studio with Mercedes, getting nowhere with her, unfortunately. According to the cop, Breton wanted to report it, but not without a translator. He came to fetch someone bilingual and found Duchamp. They went to the police station and were stuck there all night."

"So that's where he was." said Hare. "Jacqueline told me he didn't come in until nearly 8:00 a.m., and he was exhausted. He didn't even undress, just dropped into bed. She couldn't understand it. He hardly drinks, and she doesn't think he has a lover. Anyway, she wasn't going to wait around to ask him where he'd been."

Hare leaned across the table. He lowered his voice to a whisper. "What about the shipment?"

"It was supposed to arrive on Friday. I stopped by that afternoon, but Lam said it hadn't been delivered yet. He was expecting it any time."

The waitress appeared and freshened their coffees. The pause gave Hare a moment to think.

"Suppose someone followed Carlos to Lam's, waited until he dropped it off, then broke in and stole it? Maybe Lam put up a fight, and the thief killed him."

"Why wait until it was delivered?" reasoned Matta. "Why not just grab it from Carlos?"

"Because if he's out on the street he could call for help or get away. Once it's in the apartment, anyone who wanted it could go up and get it in private."

"There was no break-in."

"That means Lam opened the doors. It must have been someone he knew. No wonder the cops suspect one of his friends."

"No one but you, me, Lam and Carlos knew about the deal," Matta reminded him. "And we don't know if Carlos delivered. The cop who talked to me said nothing about robbery. Of course he told me next to nothing, just that it was not an accident or natural causes."

Matta took a sip of his coffee, and made a face. He hated the watery liquid that passed for coffee in New York. Hare stirred sugar into his.

"We need to find Carlos," he said.

SIXTEEN.

Walking west on 110th Street, Fitz and Nita discussed their interview with Madame Carmen.

"She's quite a character," said Fitz. "I guess that phony gypsy outfit goes over with her clients."

"It's not phony," Nita assured him, "she's a real gypsy. Her family's originally from Romania, but she has the kind of looks that pass for Spanish. I don't know when they got to Cuba, but that's where she was born and raised. Nobody knows how old she is, maybe she doesn't know herself. She's been here for about twenty years. She knows everybody, Cuban and otherwise. They all go to her with their troubles, which is why she's such a great source of information. She's not really a snitch—if she were, she wouldn't last long in this neighborhood—but she can point me in the right direction, make suggestions, drop a name, that sort of thing. As we were leaving, she said, 'Talk to Joey.'"

They reached the corner and Nita stopped. "Let me have a couple of those headshots. I'll go over to Joey's. If he can give me a line on Lam, I'll call you at the station."

Fitz was not at all insulted by her offer. In fact, he was relieved. He was in unfamiliar territory, had no contacts on the street, didn't speak the language. Might as well have been in a foreign country. All doors were closed to him except the ones that Nita opened.

"Thanks, Nita. You don't have to take this on, but I appreciate it. Who's Joey?"

"José Ramirez. He's a nasty little hoodlum who runs a protection racket out of a storefront on Lexington. His family moved here from Santiago de Cuba when he was a kid and opened a restaurant. Cubans are a tiny minority here, and they're very enterprising. Like my dad." She paused.

"Anyway, when Joey grew up he decided that shaking down restaurants would be more profitable, and a lot less work, than owning one. His threats are backed up by a bunch of thugs he calls a social club. They take care of collections. He also has a couple of girls on the street. It's a lucrative operation."

"Why don't you close him down?"

"No one wants to press charges. Silence may not be the best policy as far as the law is concerned, but it's the safest. These people have a lot at stake. Better to shut up and pay up than to risk a beating, a fire, or worse. So far, it's been mostly threats, some minor breakage, a couple of shopkeepers slapped around. Just enough to convince people that Joey means business. And he's smart. He doesn't squeeze too hard. He calculates how much each victim can afford. His boys do keep an eye on the clients. They never get vandalized, and nobody robs them—except Joey, that is. But he doesn't dirty his hands. Just sits behind a desk like a big shot and directs traffic."

Fitz was unimpressed. "Sounds like a two-bit punk to me. You think Lam might have had dealings with him?"

"It's a long shot, but worth checking out. Madame Carmen felt some bad vibrations, and nobody gives off more negative energy than Joey."

"You don't believe that psychic mumbo-jumbo, do you?"

"No, not really," Nita hedged. "But you can't deny that her intuition is pretty good. You saw for yourself. Her hunches, if that's what they are, sometimes pay off. Besides, I was thinking of getting onto Joey anyway. Like I said, the Cuban community is very small. If Joey doesn't know Lam, nobody around here does." She checked her watch. "It's nearly noon. I'd better get over there."

Fitz knew there was no point in his going along. It might just complicate things. "I'll go back downtown and report," he told her. "I'll be at the station in half an hour. You'll call me as soon as you can?"

Nita recognized the signal that told her his concern was more than professional.

"Of course," she replied, with a smile calculated to charm. "I won't keep you in suspense."

SEVENTEEN.

The black sedan with Connecticut license plates pulled up to the curb on 10th Street, opposite the gate that led to Patchin Place. The driver got out, unlocked the gate, and eased the car into the alley and down to number 5. The forty-mile drive from Darien had taken a little over an hour and a half. Anne Matta's father believed that his car got the best mileage at a speed of thirty or less. His wife's volunteer work as a United Service Organizations driver allowed them ample gas ration coupons, but he saw no need to waste them.

As he opened the back door for his daughter, William Clark once again stifled his dismay at the prospect of Anne and her four-month-old twins living in a second-floor walkup on a seedy dead-end street in this crummy neighborhood. Since he was paying the rent, he thought they should be someplace nicer, but Anne had convinced him that her husband needed to live near the other artists, who congregated in and around the Village. Besides, she told him, for the same rent in a better neighborhood they wouldn't have room for a studio.

She could handle the groceries and the stroller, she said. "I'll take them up first and then come back down for the boys."

They unloaded her overnight bag and the basket with the baby supplies, which Anne carried across the sidewalk, up the three steps to the front door and into the hall. Clark followed with the twins, Gordon and Sebastian, one in each arm. He wondered how Anne would manage once they started walking.

Her husband was no help. Oh, he was charming, intelligent, probably quite talented, though to Clark his paintings were ugly. He made a big fuss over the boys, bragged about how handsome they are—just like him, was the implication—but never lifted a finger to feed them or bathe them or change their diapers. But Anne was committed to him and wouldn't hear a word of criticism, so he had learned to keep his misgivings to himself.

Anne made two trips to the second-floor hall, deposited the stroller, groceries, and luggage, and returned downstairs. She took the sleeping boys from her father's arms.

"No need to come up, Dad," she told him. "I'm an old hand at this already. You get on home." She stepped toward him and stood on tiptoe for a kiss.

With the twins in her arms he couldn't embrace her as he would have liked to. He wanted to sweep her up, bundle her and the boys back into the car, and drive them home to Darien, away from this unsavory place and her feckless husband.

When she met Matta in Paris in 1938, he was a fledgling architect with a promising career ahead of him, but no sooner had she fallen in love with him than he threw it over to become a painter. What sort of prospects did that offer? Even in Paris, the center of the art world, the most advanced artists were starving, and of course Matta wanted to be one of the innovators. On top of that, the war came and they had to get out.

Clark reflected on the bright side. Thank God Matta hadn't taken her to his family in Chile! They would have been completely cut off for the duration, and she would have been among strangers, not knowing the language, totally dependent. At least here we can keep an eye on her, help with the expenses, and the twins had been born United States citizens. And they're less than an hour away by train. If things fall apart, he reasoned, she and the boys can always come to us.

"It was sweet of you and Mother to put up with us for a few days," said Anne. "It was too bad of her not to let me lift a finger, but I admit it was a nice break for me." She adjusted the twins in her arms. "These two are quite demanding."

Clark touched her cheek. "You know how much your mother and I love having you with us. You must come whenever you like and stay as long as you like." He added tactfully, "Of course Roberto is welcome whenever he can get away."

Anne was not fooled by his diplomacy. "I know how you feel about him, Dad. You think he's wasting his time painting pictures no one wants to buy, but he works hard at it and he's making headway. Peggy Guggenheim is promoting him. She has rich friends who she's trying to interest in his work. Even the Museum of Modern Art is interested. But it takes time. He's only been painting for a few years, and his ideas are kind of radical. Don't think he doesn't appreciate your support. I know you say it's a gift, not a loan, but he wants to pay you back once he gets established. I have faith in him. I hope you will, too."

They had had similar conversations before, always polite, never spinning out of control, but always ending with the same unsatisfactory stalemate. She was devoted to a man he disapproved of, and she showed no sign of changing her mind. Still, he knew better than to alienate her. His consolation was how close they were to Darien. Clark actually hoped that Matta would prove him wrong, but if not, Anne didn't have far to go.

He kissed her again, and they said their goodbyes.

Anne found the apartment door unlocked. The party guest who had slept on the couch had revived after Matta left and didn't lock up on his way out. All the other remains—the full ashtrays, the stale food, the dirty glasses—were still there. The only thing missing was her husband.

She surveyed the room with resignation, determined to have it cleaned up by the time he returned. Quickly she parked the twins in their double crib in the bedroom and fetched her things from the hall. She didn't bother to unpack. The kitchen garbage pail was spilling over, so down she went again to find an empty bin. With a window opened to air out the smell of stale cigarette smoke, and the bin in the middle of the living room floor, she got to work.

EIGHTEEN.

Collins watched as the two men came out of the coffee shop and walked toward Hare's loft. Their conversation was animated, and even though he couldn't hear what they were saying, it was clear that they were making plans of some kind. Hare gestured to himself and then poked Matta's chest with a finger. I'll do this, and you'll do that, thought Collins. He wished he knew what they had in mind, especially since they were splitting up. Hare went into the loft, and Matta turned west on Bleecker. Should I follow him, Collins asked himself, or wait to see what Hare does next? Better stick with Matta.

The artist and his tail headed up Bleecker Street to Hudson, then west on Gansevoort, toward the river. Wonder where this is leading, mused Collins. His curiosity was soon satisfied, as Matta turned onto the dock at Pier 52, where a freighter with the name *Princesa* painted on its rusting bow was taking on cargo. A crane lifted crates high in the air above the deck, and stevedores expertly maneuvered them into the hold.

The gangway was down, and more men carried supplies and provisions on board. Matta approached a crew member with a manifest who was apparently checking the stock. Slipping behind a truck loaded with waiting cargo, Collins worked his way as close to them as he dared. He was able to overhear only a few words that unfortunately were in Spanish. He saw the purser shake his head, heard him say él no está aquí, saw Matta press him, and saw the sailor's frown and even more emphatic head-shake. He clearly didn't like the interruption.

The artist reached into his pocket and extracted a pencil and a small pad. He wrote something, and tore off the sheet. From another pocket he removed a bill, folded it around the note, and handed it to the purser, who suddenly looked a lot friendlier. He nodded and spoke a few words in reply as he pocketed the paper.

Matta turned and headed back down the pier to West Street. Once or twice he looked back over his shoulder toward the ship, so Collins stayed behind the truck until Matta reached Gansevoort. He could easily keep his mark in sight from a block away, and he had a pretty good idea that Matta was now headed back to Hare's place.

Instead of taking the long walk down Bleecker, Matta decided to make his report by phone. Unlike most of the artists, for whom a private telephone was an unimaginable luxury, the well-heeled Hare had service. When Matta got to Eighth Avenue, he popped into a drugstore and used the public booth. He was in and out in five minutes and led the detective back to Patchin Place.

I'll get the beat cop to keep an eye on him, Collins decided. There was that list of Lam's friends to check out.

It was going to be a long afternoon.

NINETEEN.

When Hare returned from the coffee shop Jacqueline was still lying on the bed, her naked body displayed to advantage on the colorful Mexican serape that he used as a coverlet. At age thirty-two, more than six years Hare's senior, she was as nubile and captivating as a girl his own age. Once again he marveled at the beauty of her ivory skin, the silky blonde hair on both her head and her pubis, and the strong, supple legs that had recently been wrapped around his shoulders. Her mood did not match her appearance.

"What was so urgent that you had to run out on me?" Her frustration at their interrupted lovemaking had made her cross.

Unfortunately for her, Matta's news had indeed killed Hare's appetite for sex. Although he couldn't tell her everything, she would understand when she learned what had happened to Lam. He sat on the bed and folded the serape over her to minimize the distraction.

"I'm sorry, darling, but Matta needed to see me right away. He told me that last night, while we were enjoying ourselves at the party, Fredo was lying dead in his studio. It was André who found him. It seems someone killed him."

"Oh, no," she gasped, and her body jerked upright. Hare pulled her into his arms.

"The police came to see Matta this morning," he explained. "They're checking up on Fredo's friends. He wanted to warn me that they'll likely be coming here." He stroked her cheek and kissed her forehead.

"You should go home. André can tell you much more than I can, and the police may want to talk to you as well. It would be better if you were there, with your husband and child, don't you think?"

"Yes, of course," she agreed. "André will need me to translate if they have questions for him. And I don't want them to frighten Aube." She threw off the serape and rose from the bed to retrieve her clothes. David caught his breath as he watched her dress. Even in her distracted state, every movement was graceful.

God, how lovely she is, he thought. I must keep her out of this.

She turned to him, her expression troubled. "David, who on earth could have done this? Why would the police think it was one of us? We all loved Fredo."

He avoided her eyes. "We don't know the circumstances. They told Matta practically nothing. Anyway it must be routine to talk to friends and family when someone is killed, and his family is in Cuba, so we're the closest people to him."

Closer than you realize, he was thinking. Not only friends and fellow artists but also business partners, and in a business that I'd just as soon the police didn't find out about. That's probably what got him killed.

TWENTY.

Joey Ramirez liked to keep his office door open. He had placed his desk—in the back room of the former candy store that served as his headquarters—opposite the door so he could look through the front room to the glass entrance door and windows. That way he could see who was coming and going. and people outside could see that the boss was in his office, wearing a respectable suit and tie, looking like the successful businessman he was. Sitting behind the desk on an office chair raised to its full height also hid the fact that he was only five foot three.

Unobtrusive gold lettering on the outside door read Lexington Social Club / Members Only. The young men who lounged in the front room enforced that rule. They were also clearly visible to anyone who doubted the muscle behind Joey's organization.

The office door was closed only when Joey was in a private meeting, as he was now with Juanita Diaz.

"Welcome. Officer Diaz," he began cordially. "I haven't seen you in a while, not since that unfortunate misunderstanding with my girl Esperanza. What brings you to my social club?"

Nita placed one of the headshots on the desk. Joey picked it up and took a good look. "Who's the stiff?"

"You don't know him?"

"If I did, why would I ask?"

Lying is like breathing to him, Nita said to herself, but I don't think he recognizes Lam.

"He's a Cuban immigrant who was found dead in his Greenwich Village apartment last night," she explained. "Name of Wifredo Lam. We're trying to get a line on his associates. The local cops down there asked me to find out if he had any connections up here."

"Lam, huh? Must've had a chink father. Sure looks like it. I saw half-breeds like that in Santiago. Used to throw rocks at 'em when I was a kid." He chuckled at the memory.

"What a charming little boy you must have been, Joey," Nita cooed, emphasizing the word little. "And bright as a button, I'll bet. At the top of your reform school class, no doubt."

Joey didn't appreciate sarcasm, especially from a woman. If one of his girls sassed him like that, the next thing that came out of her mouth would be a cry of pain. But this ball-breaker was a police officer, so he masked his anger with a genial grin.

"Reform school? Not me. I've always been a law-abiding citizen. Always happy to help the police with their inquiries."

"Then ask around. Find out if anyone knew Lam, and let me know." She jotted the deceased's name on the back of the photo, together with her phone number at the precinct, and handed it back.

Nita rose to leave. She was six inches taller than Joey. He didn't get up to see her out.

TWENTY-ONE.

Carlos Solana was in a quandary. After an uncomfortable night on a sagging cot at the Seamen's Church Institute on South Street, a wash and shave with tepid water, and a breakfast of weak coffee and bland rolls in the institute's galley, he was sitting on a bench overlooking the East River, trying to decide on his next move. Using his ditty bag for a pillow had given him a stiff neck, but he was taking no chances on someone making off with it while he slept.

Finding Lam dead in the studio had shaken him badly. If only he had gotten there on Friday as planned, he could have delivered the package to his friend, picked up his money, had a delicious Cuban dinner at Little Havana, spent the night in a comfortable bed in Lam's apartment, and gone out with him on Saturday to see the sights. Then Lam wouldn't have been home when the killer arrived. But a hurricane in the Caribbean had delayed the departure from Cartagena, and the ship had arrived a day late. By the time they had berthed at Pier 52 and he was given shore leave, it was 8:45 p.m.

It had taken him less than twenty minutes to walk across the West Village to Lam's apartment. The light was on in the studio. He must be wondering where I am, thought Carlos. He had his own keys—Lam had given him a set after his first visit. "Come up any time you're in port," he had said. "even if I'm not around. The day bed in the studio is yours whenever you want it. It's not the Hotel Gran Caribe, but it makes a change from the hard bunk on that rusty tub you're stuck in most of the time." So kind and generous. Always ready to translate so Carlos wouldn't feel lost in a city where he didn't speak the language. And a great companion, full of interesting ideas.

His paintings were kind of crazy, but when he explained them you could see what he was driving at. The figures weren't supposed to look real, like the pinups over Carlos's bunk. Sometimes they were sexy, but not like pretty girls, more like she-devils that would put a spell on you.

Playing that silly drawing game with Lam helped him understand. You couldn't tell where it would lead or what kind of picture you'd end up with, but it was bound to be something really strange. Something magical. With his fantastic imagination, Lam could develop one of those little drawings into a whole world on canvas. "They are the matches that light my fire," he said.

"No more matches." Carlos murmured in Spanish. "and no more deal." Lam was dead, and he still had the package. but no idea what the next step was supposed to be.

TWENTY-TWO.

Joey pressed a button on his desk and a bell rang in the front room. The five gang members playing blackjack looked at one another and at their hands.

"Low hand goes," said one of them. Raul Gutierrez, a weedy specimen whose chief asset was unquestioning loyalty to Joey, had a deuce and a five. He threw in his cards, forfeited his stake, and left the table to answer his boss's summons.

Joey handed him the photograph of Lam. "Ever seen this guy?"

Raul frowned at the picture. "Not when he was alive."

"Half chink, half chardo. Somebody iced him downtown. That cunt cop who just pranced out wants me to get a line on him. I'm feeling civic-minded, so I said okay."

Joey's real motivation was somewhat more self-serving. If Lam had been killed over a deal with someone in his territory, he wanted to know who, what and why. There might be something in it for him.

"You want me to ask around?" Raul suggested.

"No, asshole, I want you to stay here and circle-jerk with that bunch of fairies out front."

"Sorry, boss. I'll get right on it."

70

"Call me if you come up with anything. No, not if, when."

After showing Lam's photo to the rest of the gang and drawing a blank, Raul spent what was left of the morning canvassing every shop and restaurant in the neighborhood, with the same result. He called from a pay phone to report.

"Keep looking," Joey ordered.

Suddenly Raul had one of his rare ideas. "You said he was killed downtown, right?"

"Yeah, that's where he lived. An apartment in the Village, she said."

"I got an uncle owns a bar down there. Okay if I ask him?"

"Nothing to lose, right? But don't take all day. And no drinking on the job, understand?"

Raul headed for the IRT subway station at 110th Street. Two transfers later, he emerged at 14th Street and Seventh Avenue, not far from where West Street intersects Horatio. That was his destination.

Sunday afternoon

TWENTY-THREE.

The Port of Call stood in a row of grubby commercial buildings on West Street, in the Express Highway's shadow, facing the North River docks. The name was neatly lettered on a plywood panel that covered what once had been a plate glass window, and a small neon sign over the door said simply BAR. Inside, the atmosphere was strictly utilitarian. No nautical-themed decorations, no hatch-cover tabletops. The men who drank here needed no reminders of life at sea. The customers were almost exclusively the ships' crews, as well as the stevedores, longshoremen, and truckers who serviced the freighters.

Raul's uncle Julio commuted to the Port of Call every day from uptown. He opened at noon. Arriving not long after opening time, Raul found the place nearly deserted. His uncle was at his usual station behind the bar, crating empty beer bottles for pickup.

"¡Buenos tardes, Raulito!" cried Julio with delight as his nephew approached. "¿Cómo estuvo tu día?"

"Not so hot, tio. I got a problem. Joey wants me to get a line on a Cuban guy, but I'm coming up empty." Raul pulled out the photo. "This guy ever come in here? He lived in the Village."

Julio shook his head. "No, I don't think so. Not a sailor, right? And not living in the Village any more. In fact, not living at all."

"You got that right. This photo was taken at the morgue. Somebody snuffed him last night. Joey wants to know why."

Julio flipped the photo. "Funny name, Wifredo Lam. Cuban, you say?"

A man rose from the far end of the bar and approached them. "Let me have a look," he said. He turned the photo to the light. "Yeah, that's Lam all right. He's a friend of one of my shipmates."

Raul couldn't hide his enthusiasm. "Now we're getting somewhere! What do you know about him?"

The seaman eyed him steadily. "I know plenty, but why should I tell you?"

"No reason," replied Raul. "But maybe you'll tell my buddy Abe." He opened his wallet and laid a five-dollar bill on the bar.

"I'll tell him and his twin brother."

Raul placed another five on top of the first one. The seaman picked them up and folded them into the pocket of his pea jacket. He didn't offer his name, and Raul didn't press him. Let him play it his way, he said to himself. He asked his uncle to draw a couple of beers, and he took them to a table.

"Good health," he said, lifting his glass. "I'm sure glad I ran into you."

"Your lucky day," replied his companion. They drank in silence for a few minutes.

"About a year ago," the seaman began, "we were making our regular run from Cartagena to New York with a cargo of coffee. Not many freighters do the Atlantic coast route these days, but our owners are willing to take the risk if the profits are high enough. On the way we called in at Mariel to pick up Cuban rum and cigars. Always get a good

73

return on that cargo. We picked up a passenger, too. That was Lam.

"He gets to talking with the crew, and it turns out he's from the same town in Cuba as my mate Carlos. They really hit it off, spent a lot of time together. Carlos let him come into the crew's quarters and use the table for sketching. Lam's an artist. He had a little watercolor set, some pencils and paper on him, the rest of his gear was in the hold.

"He gave Carlos drawing lessons, but the stuff they did was kind of weird. They'd fold up the paper and hand it back and forth. Carlos showed me a couple, and they looked all jumbled. Lam said that was the point. His kind of art was supposed to look like something you'd only see in your dreams. I said it looked more like a nightmare, and he said, 'You're right, that's what I been through.'

"He told us that before the war he'd been doing pretty well in France, but his crowd got kicked out by the Nazis. They had to hide out in Marseilles, waiting for a ship and hoping the Gestapo didn't find them before they could scram. Him and his wife managed to make it to Cuba, but there was no support for him there. He decided to park his wife with his family and try his luck in New York. He said his pals from Paris are sitting out the war here and they got friends with money who are helping them out."

"How long ago was that?"

"Like I said, around this time last year. Yeah, fall of '42. When we dock in New York, him and Carlos go off together. Carlos don't speak no English, but Lam's was pretty good. They went to look up one of Lam's artist friends, a Chilean guy lives in the Village. He put Lam up for a few days and found him a place in the neighborhood.

"From then on, whenever we got into port Carlos would go straight over there and hang out with Lam. He'd come back with great stories about the crazy artists he met."

74

The seaman paused and finished his beer. Raul signaled his uncle for a refill.

"Something he said last time, maybe you should know. He comes back to the ship grinning from ear to ear. I says, 'You pick a winning number?' 'Better,' he says, 'this ain't no gamble. It's a sure thing.' 'What gives?' I says, and he tells me he's got a business deal with Lam that's gonna pay off big. That's all he'd say."

"I need to talk to Carlos."

The seaman shook his head. "He ain't on board now. Has shore leave while we unload and take on cargo, so he went to Lam's. That was yesterday. If Lam's dead, he ain't there, so I don't know where he could be. But he has to be back on board by tonight. We ship out first thing Monday morning."

Raul pulled out the notebook and pencil with which he recorded protection payments. "Give me some details, man. What's Carlos's last name? What does he look like? What's the name of your ship, and where is it docked? What time do you leave port on Monday?"

"I kinda forget those things. I think Abe could jog my memory."

Reluctantly, Raul opened his wallet again and extracted another five. This time he laid it on the table and covered it with his left hand while he flipped open the notebook with his right. "Abe is asking," he prompted.

The seaman gave him the information and drained his glass. Raul took his hand off the bill, which disappeared into the pea-jacket pocket.

TWENTY-FOUR.

Carlos was feeling increasingly desperate. After buying a hot dog from a street vendor, he was down to his last few coins. His pay went directly into the Seamen's Bank for Savings on Wall Street, where the shipping company had its account, but the bank was closed on Sunday. He could have drawn something on account from the ship's purser, but he'd expected to have a pocketful of folding money by Saturday night, so he didn't bother. Of course he could go back on board, but the undelivered package was burning a hole in his ditty bag.

He had trusted Lam to make the arrangements. All he knew was that someone would hand him a package in Cartagena and that he was to pay the man $100 American. Lam had given him the cash the last time he was in New York.

"When you bring me the package." he had told Carlos, "a fellow I know will pay you $300 for it. You go back to Cartagena, pay a hundred for another package, and keep the other two hundred."

Lam had smiled broadly and clapped him on the back. "Not bad money for a delivery boy."

Not bad at all. More money, in fact, than Carlos made in a month at sea. It had seemed so easy, and in fact it was. The contact that met him as he debarked in Cartagena had greeted him like an old friend, whisked him off to a nearby cantina and, over a glass of guaro, handed off the package in exchange for the envelope of cash. Carlos had gone straight back to the ship and stashed it in the hidey-hole under his bunk. He didn't trust his sea chest—too many of his shipmates were good at picking locks. He made the secret cache after a box of contraband cigars went missing from the chest before he could sell them on the New York docks, where the longshoremen were ready customers for smuggled goods.

The contents of this package could not be peddled piecemeal like cigars. It was medical-grade Peruvian cocaine, a kilo of it.

With all the legal production diverted to the military and smuggling riskier than ever due to the threat of U-boat attacks, the drug's price had increased significantly in the past couple of years. Carlos had no idea how much it was worth uncut to a dealer, but its street value would be many times the three hundred that Lam's contact was paying. Yet it was worth nothing to Carlos if he couldn't pass it on.

It could be worse than worthless. Suppose Lam's body had been discovered and the police were investigating? Suppose they had connected him with Lam, and were looking for him? If they found the package on him he'd be sunk. He thought about dumping it in the East River, but the prospect of throwing away $300 made him reconsider.

Maybe I could go to Matta, that Chilean pal of Lam's, he thought. He lives right down the block from Lam.

He started walking north toward 10th Street, but began having second thoughts along the way. How could the artist possibly help him? He wasn't likely to have a spare three hundred just lying around, so he wasn't going to take the stuff off Carlos's hands. And how could he explain the whole business? What if the guy called the cops?

Then he remembered that, before he met up with Lam and Matta, when he first sailed into New York harbor not knowing anyone in the city, one of his shipmates had taken him to East Harlem, where the bartenders and waiters spoke Spanish and there were even a few Cubans sprinkled in among the mostly Puerto Rican population.

As they were enjoying a couple of cold Hatueys at the Agozar, his buddy pointed out one of them, a short young man in a sharp suit, arguing with a brassy girl at the bar.

"Hard to believe," his buddy said, "but that little runt is the big cheese around here. He runs the rackets out of the shop next door. Looks like one of his whores is holding out on him. If you want to make some extra cash, Joey's always in the market for Cuban smokes and booze."

Carlos fished in his trouser pocket and found a nickel for the Third Avenue El.

TWENTY-FIVE.

Raul dropped a dime in the pay phone next to the Port of Call men's room and dialed the Lexington Social Club number. The phone was answered in the front room.

"It's me, Raul. Tell Joey to pick up."

It was a few moments before the extension was picked up and Raul heard the other receiver disconnect. The boys weren't too curious about his errand.

"What have you got?"

"Good news, boss. It took some doing and it cost three fins and three beers, but I got a line on Lam that ties him to a merchant seaman who makes a regular run to South America." He didn't mention that his meeting with Carlos's shipmate had been dumb luck. "From what my contact told me," he continued, "I think Lam and this sailor were working a smuggling racket."

Joey interrupted him before he could give the details. "Sailor name of Carlos Solana, off the *Princesa* out of Cartagena, right?"

Raul almost dropped the receiver. "How the fuck do you know that?"

"I know because before I took your call Carlos Solana, able seaman, was standing in my office holding a key of what he says is pure coke. He was supposed to deliver the stuff to Lam, but he got there too late."

"No shit! How did he get to you?"

"He heard I was the man," said Joey enigmatically. "Right now the bundle is on my desk and Carlos is cooling his heels in the front room. You can come back, I got all the information I need."

After he rang off, Joey took a switchblade out of the desk drawer and made a small hole in the package. He moistened a fingertip and inserted it. It came away with a coating of white powder, which he rubbed on his gums. A smile lit up his face. "Excelente," he murmured.

Properly cut, this could be worth as much as $3,000 on the street. Maybe more if he could connect to one or two of the midtown nightclubs. Pulling a roll of Scotch tape out of the drawer, he repaired the hole. He pressed the call button, and Carlos was escorted back into the office. His distress was obvious.

"Please, take a seat," said Joey affably in Spanish, indicating a chair in front of the desk. Carlos sank into it.

"How would you like to join our little social club?" he offered. "We could use a South American chapter."

"What would I have to do?" Carlos asked warily.

"Same as what you just did." Joey put his hand on the package. "Pick up another one just like this in Cartagena and deliver it to me. You do that, and you get five hundred American every time. Out of that, you pay whatever the goods cost wholesale and you keep the rest."

Carlos could hardly believe it. This was an even better deal than he had with Lam. Same risk, but a much greater reward. He wanted to jump at it, but there was a catch.

"You are very generous, sir. I would like nothing more than to join your club, but I do not see how I can do what you ask. The contact in Cartagena was arranged for me, I have no idea how. He came to the dock, gave me the goods, I paid him a hundred American, and he left. How will I find him again?"

Joey chuckled. "If he wants another hundred, he will find you." He unlocked a drawer, took out ten fifty-dollar bills, and handed them to Carlos.

"Next time, give him a hundred and fifty."

TWENTY-SIX.

By the time Collins got back to the station, Fitz had already returned from Harlem and was waiting in Collins's office. "Any luck uptown?" asked the detective.

Yes, Fitz thought, considering that he had met Nita, but he shook his head. "Not yet, sir, but Officer Diaz is following up. She'll ask around and report."

"That's the best we can do in that neighborhood," replied Collins. "O'Connell said he would investigate the possible Chinatown connection. He has a contact."

Collins settled in behind his desk. He leaned on his elbows and stared past Fitz toward the far distance. "This case sure is a peculiar one," he reflected. "I don't mind telling you it gives me the creeps."

"I know what you mean, sir," agreed Fitz. "Diaz and I went to see a Cuban fortune teller to find out if she recognized Lam. She had a couple of premonitions, I guess you'd call 'em, that were pretty much on target. She kind of ran her hands over the crime scene photo and asked where his wife was. Said she felt a woman's presence, but the wife's in Cuba, and I never mentioned him being married."

"Did she say anything about that get-up he was wearing?"

"Just that it wasn't anything to do with Cuban voodoo, what they call Santería. She said that, according to their belief, it would be sacrilegious to do that to a dead body. But maybe that was the point. Maybe he had a run-in with one of their priests and the outfit was meant to show disrespect."

Collins sighed deeply. "Jesus, that's all we need, a ritual killing involving a weird religion. I sure hope it turns out to be something straightforward, like a jealous husband. Right now we don't even know how he was killed, much less why."

He glanced at the wall clock. "Maybe I should call the medical examiner and see if he can hurry up that damned autopsy report." If there was a backlog at the morgue, Lam might be at the end of a long line.

The intercom buzzed, and Sergeant Ryan notified the detective that there was a reporter in the lobby asking for details about the murder investigation.

Collins was indignant. "One of these days I'll find out who around here the *Daily News* is paying off," he growled.

Quick to defend his fellow officers, Fitz speculated. "Probably someone at the morgue, sir, or the photo lab."

"In that case, the son of a bitch probably already has the crime scene shots. Just the sort of lurid stuff 'New York's Picture Newspaper' loves. If he does, we'll know where the tip-off came from."

Collins grunted as he rose, resigned to the impending ordeal. So little was known that his answers to the obvious questions—cause of death, motive, and suspects—would seem evasive, or worse. He could imagine the headline: *Voodoo Killing Stumps Police*.

TWENTY-SEVEN.

The interview with the *Daily News* reporter was mercifully brief. He didn't have the telltale photograph, only the victim's name and a bare outline of the case. Collins was able to verify that two friends had found Wifredo Lam, an artist, dead on the floor of his apartment at 140 West 10th Street at around 11:00 last night. Time of death uncertain. Cause of death unknown, pending the autopsy. Suspicious? Possibly. No, murder couldn't be ruled out, but couldn't be confirmed at this stage. Unwise to speculate. No apparent break-in, no apparent robbery.

"Listen," said Collins, leaning in confidentially, "do you mind holding off until we can notify the next of kin? It would be terrible for them if they learned about his death by reading the paper." He failed to mention that Lam's family was far outside the circulation area of the *Daily News*.

With little solid information to go on, and with Collins's assurance that he would call as soon as the family was told, the reporter agreed to wait. On the face of it, this didn't seem like much of a story. Guy might have had a heart attack, or choked to death on his dinner. People drop dead all the time.

The reporter handed Collins his card and left.

"I hope the door didn't hit him in the ass on the way out," Ryan mumbled from behind the desk.

"Heavens, no. We wouldn't want a lawsuit on our hands." Collins chuckled as he made his way down the hall. Back in his office, he pulled the list of Lam's friends they'd gotten from Duchamp and Matta. He took it out to the desk and handed it to the clerk on duty.

"Jeff, I want you to check the city directory and verify as many of these addresses as you can. You can try the phone book, too, but I doubt they have service. I'm going for a bite of lunch, maybe half an hour. I'd appreciate it if you could have the list for me when I get back."

"Yes, sir, not a problem," said the clerk obligingly.

"Shouldn't take long." There were only about a dozen names. Some had only the street, not the building number, but that narrowed it down. The list, neatly typed, was waiting for Collins when he returned.

"You were right, sir," said the clerk. "Only two of 'em have phones—that Hare fella over on Bleecker and a guy named Motherwell on 8th Street. The others must communicate by smoke signal."

"They're all artists," replied Collins. "They probably draw pictures for each other. They got their own language. Damned if I understand it. The whole business is baffling."

He took the list and studied it a moment. "Well, maybe these folks can shed some light. I'd better go find out."

TWENTY-EIGHT.

When he stepped out of the Lexington Social Club, Carlos Solana was holding more money than he earned in two months of deck work on the *Princesa*. He went next door to the Agozar, ordered a beer, a sandwich, and a pack of Camels, and broke one of the fifties. The remaining nine didn't even make a bulge in the inside pocket of his pea jacket, but they did make him very nervous. He decided to take the subway straight back to the ship and stash them in his hidey-hole, then stay on board until they shoved off.

Thank God he no longer had the incriminating package, so much harder to conceal and protect. His neck was still stiff from sleeping on it. Everything would be simpler next time. Now he was dealing with an organization, not a single person. Joey was going to set up a contact at the North River docks that would know when the ship was due and if there was a delay.

Sometimes they had to lay over when there was a U-boat alert, or bad weather, like this time. These last-minute schedule changes didn't always show up in the published shipping news, but the longshoremen waiting to unload cargo were informed by ship-to-shore radio. The contact would meet the ship, collect the package, and pay him off there and then. He wouldn't even have to carry the goods uptown.

Smuggling came naturally to Carlos and his shipmates. They always carried some contraband, small things they could sell in port for a bit of extra spending money. A few months ago, Carlos had brought in some Cuban cigars and held back a couple for himself and Lam. That was how the idea got started.

Lam had asked him, "What else do you carry?" "Sometimes rum," he answered. "Once, an emerald that my cousin told me he found." On his next visit, Lam said that a friend had connections in Peru that could supply something really valuable and easy to carry. If he was interested, there was good money in it.

Carlos was interested. Even more so now. On the subway ride downtown, he thought about his prospects. Thanks to Joey, he was going to be rich. His only regret was that it was Lam's death that sent him to the Lexington Social Club.

Suddenly, he was overcome by a longing for his friend's company. He wanted to share the news of his good fortune, but he wouldn't have had this luck if Lam were alive. It was a sad paradox.

If giving up the extra hundred and fifty—or even two hundred, if he ignored Joey's advice—could have brought Lam back to life, Carlos would have done it gladly. At least that's what he told himself for comfort.

TWENTY-NINE.

Frustrated and increasingly nervous, Matta returned to Patchin Place. Two doors stood between him and his apartment. The outside door was locked, and he cursed under his breath as he fumbled for the key. By the time he had climbed to the second floor, he was all in. Another locked door, another irritating delay while he found the apartment key. As he stumbled inside, he met the anxious eyes of his wife, who had just finished rolling the living room carpet back into place.

The sight of her startled him. He had completely forgotten that she and the boys were due back from her parents' house today.

"Darling," cried Anne, "where have you been? You look like you're about to drop!"

He walked past her in a daze and collapsed onto the couch. She knelt in front of him and took both his hands in hers. "Let me get you some coffee. Have you had anything to eat? Here, give me your coat."

"Don't fuss so," he snapped. "I just need some rest. My head is splitting." He stretched out and covered his eyes with his hands.

Just then one of the twins let out a squeal and began to whimper. Matta winced. "Can't you keep those brats quiet?"

Anne rushed into the bedroom and swept up Sebastian, the offending infant. His brother, Gordon, still fast asleep, must have been restless and poked or kicked him. Thankfully he calmed down right away. Sometimes they set each other off and there was a double dose of bawling.

She settled Sebastian and went back to tend to the cranky baby in the living room. But he was already out cold.

THIRTY.

Still wearing Max Ernst's silk pajamas and now sporting his cashmere bathrobe and kidskin slippers as well, Duchamp shuffled into Peggy's kitchen in search of something to eat. In her efforts to charm her errant husband, the newly minted Mrs. Ernst had spared no expense on his nightclothes, but neglected to consider his nutritional needs. The breadbox was empty, and the icebox held nothing but two bottles of champagne. Duchamp opened the cupboard doors, hopeful of finding a box of the Ritz crackers that were Peggy's favorite support for canapés, but was disappointed. Fortunately there was some coffee, and he busied himself with it as she joined him.

"Peggy, my dear, you really must stock your larder with a few staples," he scolded. "Not even a mouse could find sustenance here."

"Of course you're right, Luigi," she admitted. "But you know I never cook any more. When I lived with Douglas Garman at Yew Tree Cottage I cooked all the meals—he was as helpless in the kitchen as he was clever in the garden. Max is an excellent cook, but he's never here. Now I eat every meal out and have even forgotten how to boil water. I'm so glad you have taken charge of the coffee. I'll send Louisa out for some pastries. Or would you rather have bread and cheese?"

Duchamp had strong opinions on the subject. "I prefer not to eat any cheese I don't buy myself. Likewise, American bread must be chosen very carefully."

"But there's an authentic boulangerie not two blocks from here! It is also a pâtisserie. It belongs to the pastry chef from the French pavilion at the recent international exposition. He simply stayed on after war was declared. Fortunately for us."

"In that case, a baguette, and perhaps some fruit confit, would be most welcome," said Duchamp with relief. "I have not eaten since late last night, when the police gave us some unspeakable coffee and things they called sinkers. An apt description, believe me."

Once the maid was dispatched and the coffee prepared, the conversation returned to last night's shocking discovery. They had already discussed it in bed, but now it was time to plan the next moves.

"Someone must notify his parents and Helena," said Peggy. "I have an address, a poste restante in Havana, but perhaps I can contact the embassy. It would be better if someone could tell them in person."

Duchamp was doubtful. "But what can they tell except that he is dead? We do not know how he died."

"Commissioner Valentine will keep me informed. There will be an autopsy, of course. You say Breton had no idea what killed him?"

"There was nothing obvious, no apparent wound, no blood. But we could not examine him. Breton thinks he may have been strangled or knocked unconscious and smothered. His face was hidden by the mask." Despite himself, Duchamp shuddered at the memory of his friend's humiliated body.

"Did the police ask you about the mask and the other, ah, decorations?"

"Yes, but I pleaded ignorance. Breton almost gave it away, but I did not translate correctly what he said. If they

91

had understood the significance, it would have pointed to one of us."

"But my dear Luigi," Peggy replied, "that is exactly where it does point."

THIRTY-ONE.

The apartment at 46 East 8th Street was a fifth-floor walkup over a printing shop. "I sure hope the others aren't all on the top floor," Collins muttered under his breath. The buzzer marked "5-Pollock" was answered, and he trudged up the dingy staircase. In the hall, a slim auburn-haired woman stood in the doorway and regarded him quizzically as he approached.

"Mrs. Pollock?" he asked politely.

"Lee Krasner," she answered, rather sharply, as if his mistake had been an insult.

He recognized the name as another on his list. Better not start off on the wrong foot by asking what she was doing in Pollock's apartment instead of her own on the next block.

"Is Mr. Pollock in? I'd like to speak to both of you."

"What for?" she said abruptly. "Who are you?"

Collins identified himself and displayed his shield. Lee eyed it dispassionately, masking her concern. She was used to dealing with the police when she collected Jackson from the drunk tank after one of his regular benders. But this was the first time a cop—a plain-clothes one at that— had shown up at the apartment. What sort of damage could her boyfriend have done to warrant a personal visit?

"Pollock's not up yet." She started to close the door.

Damn, she's prickly, thought Collins. Why so defensive, I wonder? I could come on strong and insist on seeing them both right now, or try to soften her up. He decided on the latter tactic.

"Then perhaps you'll be good enough to give me a few moments of your time," he said soothingly. "I'd really appreciate your help. May I come in?"

The effect was to pique Lee's curiosity. It didn't sound as though there'd been a complaint against Jackson, so what was it all about? She opened the door and led the detective into the kitchen. There was a pot of coffee on the gas ring, but only one cup on the table. Lee sat down and lighted a cigarette. She didn't offer one to Collins, or ask if he wanted coffee or invite him to sit, which he did anyway.

He was used to this sort of rudeness, since most of the people he interviewed were not happy to see him and only wanted him gone—unless they were crime victims, who usually were in no condition to be hospitable. In any case, he wasn't there to socialize.

Just then the bedroom door opened and a slightly groggy man in his early thirties, wearing paint-stained jeans and an untucked shirt, shambled into the kitchen, trying vainly to smooth what little hair remained on his balding head. Just in time for lunch, mused Collins, glancing at his watch. It was nearly 1:00 p.m.

"I heard voices," he mumbled then did a double take at finding a strange man in his apartment. "Who's this?" he asked Lee.

"A detective from the 6th Precinct," she answered. "He wants to talk to both of us, but he hasn't told me why. You're just in time to find out." She turned a gimlet eye on Collins, obviously his cue.

The conversation was relatively brief. Collins gave as little information as possible and got very little in return. Jackson found an empty cup, filled it with coffee, sat down at the table, groped in his shirt pocket for cigarettes and matches, and smoked in silence.

Lee did the talking. Asked if they were acquainted with Wifredo Lam, she said yes. According to her, neither she nor Jackson knew him very well, mostly ran into him at the art gallery on 57th Street where their work was shown.

How about socially? "Sometimes," she told him, "he would be at Matta's place when we made plans to reinvent Surrealism and played that silly drawing game with the folded paper." Lam enjoyed it, but she and Jackson didn't go for it. "Too contrived," said Lee. Jackson didn't contradict her.

Collins had no idea what she was talking about. His only concern was finding out who might want Lam dead. When he asked if, to their knowledge, Lam had any enemies, the creases in Jackson's forehead deepened and Lee came to attention in her chair.

"Has something happened to him?" she asked.

Without being specific, Collins told them that Lam had been found dead in his apartment and that he was investigating the circumstances.

"What the hell do you mean by 'found dead'?" demanded Lee.

Collins answered that apparently Lam had been killed by person or persons unknown, which is why he was questioning the artist's friends.

Pollock finally spoke. "Shit," he said indignantly, "why the fuck would one of his friends kill him?"

"If I talk to his friends," explained Collins patiently, "maybe I can find out if he had an enemy, and that might be the person who killed him."

"You're sure it wasn't an accident?"

"Yes, we're sure." Collins didn't elaborate.

Sunday evening

THIRTY-TWO.

"Come." barked O'Connell in response to the knock on his office door. It was 8:00 p.m., and the detective sergeant had just come back on duty.

"Here's the M.E.'s report on Lam, sir," said Jeff, the clerk, handing him a manila envelope. "Just came in. And there's a message for you from Commissioner Valentine."

O'Connell made a sour face. "Probably wants to invite me over for tea."

"Oh. no. sir." said Jeff, missing the sarcasm. "It's about the Lam case. He's taken a personal interest. Wants you to do your utmost to find the killer as quickly as possible."

Struggling to keep his temper under control. O'Connell seethed internally. He didn't want the clerk to see how insulted he was. As if he wouldn't do his utmost without the commissioner looking over his shoulder. As if he wouldn't solve the case as soon as he could without being told. He gritted his teeth. "I appreciate the commissioner's concern and will keep him apprised. Call his office with a message to that effect."

"I'm off duty now. sir. I'll get Billy to handle it."

"Good. And have him bring me the interview reports. Who else is on the case?"

"Collins has been talking to Lam's friends, and Fitzgerald went uptown to check on the Cubans, find out if he had anything going there. Nothing on that so far. I think Collins is still around if you want to see him." O'Connell allowed as how he did.

The clerk intercepted Collins on the way out. "Can you spare a minute for the boss? He just got the Lam autopsy results, in record time, too, but he's in a black mood. He wasn't real happy to learn that the commissioner has his nose in the case. Wants the boss to get his skates on. Probably lit a fire under the medical examiner, too."

"Brother, that's all we need," said Collins sympathetically. "I'll go in and offer my condolences. Besides, I'd like to know what the autopsy turned up."

A knock on the office door, followed by a growled acknowledgment, brought Collins face to face with one very irritated detective sergeant. Collins decided to lighten things up a bit, or at least try. "Jeff tells me you've received a Valentine and it isn't even February," he quipped.

"Very funny," grumbled O'Connell. "How does he even know about the case? What gripes me is—oh, never mind." He sighed with resignation. "Let's look at the post mortem."

The report described the body of Wifredo Óscar de la Concepción Lam y Castilla, a slender but well-nourished male, colored, age 40 (DOB 12-8-02), height 73 inches, weight 155 pounds. No gross abnormalities of viscera. They scanned to the bottom of the page. Dark bruise at base of skull, approximately three inches in diameter, left side, just above the hairline. Cause of death: acute epidural hematoma, the result of blunt trauma to the left occipital bone. This was the finding of Milton Helpern, M.D., Deputy Chief Medical Examiner.

"A blow to the back of the head," said Collins. "No wonder it wasn't evident. The fatal damage was internal. His hair covered the bruise."

"Then it was a deliberate assault, but who hit him, and why? Was it premeditated, or impulsive? Damn, I wish we knew if anything was stolen. Maybe we could have one of his friends on that list Matta gave you look over the apartment, see if something's missing."

No sooner had O'Connell suggested it than he reconsidered. "Wait, they're our prime suspects."

THIRTY-THREE.

Collins pulled out his notebook. "I interviewed most of 'em this afternoon," he reported. "They all seemed pretty shocked, but that's easy to fake."

O'Connell reviewed the options. "It had to be someone he knew. Either they had keys, or he let them in. If it wasn't robbery, and it looks like it wasn't, then my money's on jealousy. He was porking one of the wives or girlfriends."

"There's a few lookers on the list," Collins offered. "The Matter dame for one. Her first name's Mercedes, married to a photographer name of Herbert. They live up in Tudor City. The husband wasn't at the party, doesn't socialize much. Doesn't talk much, either. Didn't look like the jealous type to me, but she's the sort you'd want to keep an eye on if she was your wife. A real hot number."

O'Connell's eyebrows went up.

"But not my type," Collins added quickly. "I like a little more meat on the bones. Anyway, Willem de Kooning, the Dutchman down on Carmine, he's got a girlfriend I wouldn't kick out of bed for being too skinny. A young one, too, Elaine Fried. She was there when I showed up. Said she lives with her parents in Brooklyn, but it was too late to go home alone after the party so her boyfriend kindly let her crash at his place. Yeah, pull the other one, I'm thinking. The Dutchman's a lot older, small but tough looking, could be the possessive kind.

"The real knockout is the blonde who's married to the guy that found the body," he continued. "She went to the party without her husband, so I paid her a call. She's French, but speaks good English. According to her, he was working late, like he told us, or rather like that Duchamp fella told us for him. So she went on her own, and says she never even noticed him come to collect Duchamp.

"The next time she saw him was at 8:00 this morning, when he headed straight to bed and went out like a light. But he must have filled her in before he fell asleep, 'cause she wasn't at all taken aback when I told her Lam was dead.

"I tell you, boss, she is something. Drop-dead gorgeous, the athletic type. I spotted a trapeze rigged up in the front room, and she said she's an acrobat."

"Suppose Breton didn't just stumble on Lam's body," O'Connell speculated. "Suppose his wife, what's her name? —Jacqueline, thanks—is practicing her acrobatics in Lam's bed. Breton gets wise, and settles his hash. Then he comes to us with his fairy tale."

Collins considered the theory. "Then how do you explain the costume, Jack?"

"He's trying to divert us, make us think it's a Cuban cult killing. Or maybe it is."

THIRTY-FOUR.

Yun Gee waited until he knew O'Connell would be back on duty before he called the 6th Precinct. Not having his own phone, he used the booth in the corner drugstore. "I talked to the On Leong boss," he reported. "He knows Lam. He says I will be informed."

"Good work, Yun," replied O'Connell. "I know this wasn't easy for you. I hope this helps us find Lam's killer, and if it does, it'll be thanks to you."

Gee hesitated, then tried to explain the situation to the detective. "If On Leong was involved, the boss already knows all about it. It was hard to tell, his voice and his manner gave nothing away, but I don't think so. If another tong was responsible, the boss will find out why. Then he'll decide what to do. In that case I don't think he'll come back to me because I said I want justice, not revenge."

O'Connell pondered this information. "Are you telling me that if a rival tong was responsible, On Leong will settle the score without involving the authorities?"

Gee was relieved that the detective understood what he was saying. He didn't want to explain how the elaborate structure of rivalries, territorial disputes, and factional loyalties operated in Chinatown. The point was—and O'Connell had perceived this—that if Lam was dealing with a tong, the matter was out of police hands.

"When it's settled, someone will get word to me," said Gee. "When I know, you'll know."

"Listen, Yun, I don't want you to stick your neck out," O'Connell cautioned. "You have a family to think of. But if it turns out that one of the tongs was responsible for Lam's death, I want to know why he was killed. Do you think they'll tell you that?"

Even though O'Connell couldn't see it, Gee shook his head. "No," he said.

Sunday night

THIRTY-FIVE.

Officer Fitzgerald had changed into his street clothes and was just clocking out when the night man, Sergeant Flynn, called to him from the desk. "You're wanted on the phone, Fitz. It's Diaz from the 23rd."

He felt himself flush slightly and turned away as he took the receiver. "Fitzgerald here," he said, as evenly as he could. Not that Flynn was fooled.

"Glad I caught you, Fitz. Joey came through for us, though he doesn't know it." Nita was being deliberately cryptic.

"What do you mean?"

"How about I explain in person?" she offered. Fitz's heart did a little dance. "I'm off duty. I'll meet you, where?"

Inspiration struck Fitz. "Can you come downtown?" he asked, and she agreed. "Let's meet at the Cedar Tavern, 55 West 8th Street. Take your time, I'll be waiting," he told her.

"See you soon," she replied, with enough enthusiasm in her voice to tell Fitz that this meeting wasn't going to be all business.

At the Cedar, a West Village watering hole that was a popular hangout for artists, Fitz ordered a Knickerbocker and positioned himself in a booth where he could watch the entrance. His were not the only eyes that brightened when Nita arrived. As he rose to greet her and escort her to the booth, the men at the bar were visibly disappointed. "Lucky dog" was clearly written on their faces.

Out of uniform they looked like just another young couple on a date. Maybe a bit better dressed than the local clientele, more like the folks from the outer boroughs who came in to rub elbows with the art crowd, or the occasional tourists soaking up the bohemian atmosphere. Not much of that on a Sunday evening.

A few regulars were clustered at a round table in one corner, deep in a conversation notable for its unusually subdued and serious tone. Although Fitz and Nita didn't know them by sight, they were on Collins's list of Lam's friends and were discussing his mysterious death.

The two police officers sat opposite each other, and Fitz asked Nita what she wanted to drink. "What you're having is fine," she said. He ordered another Knick. He was glad she didn't want whiskey or gin—he didn't like to see a woman drinking the hard stuff. There'd been too much of that in his family. One of his aunts was a dipso, and his grandmother on his father's side had died of drink.

As for the men, they often turned to the bottle whenever problems arose and even when they didn't. Fitz's father, a captain at the 59th Precinct in Long Island City, was the exception. He'd taken the pledge when his mother died. Fitz privately vowed that if he ever felt himself going overboard, he'd join his dad on the water wagon.

He sipped his beer and gazed appreciatively at Nita. "Now," he said with a grin, "what's the word?"

"I saw Joey and gave him the picture. He said he didn't recognize Lam, but he agreed to ask around. He got one of his gang to do the legwork, and the guy hit the jackpot. He was bragging about it in the Agozar—that's the bar and grill next door to the so-called social club where

Joey has his headquarters—and Luis, the owner, called me. I had stopped in there before going to Joey's and showed Lam's picture to Luis, but he didn't know him. Neither did anyone else in the neighborhood, according to Joey's stooge, Raul."

"Then how did he track him down?"

"It happens that Raul has an uncle who owns a bar in the West Village, over by the docks. The Port of Call— you must know it, it's on your patch. I told Joey that Lam lived in the Village, so Raul decides to show the picture to his uncle. Sure enough, he IDs Lam, says he was close with a sailor off one of the freighters in port right now." Raul's self-serving version left out the coincidental meeting with the anonymous shipmate and the fact that the sailor in question had found Joey, rather than the other way around.

"This turns out to be very good news for Joey," continued Nita, "because Lam and the sailor had a deal going that fell through when Lam got killed. Now, thanks to Raul, Joey is taking over, and there's going to be a big payday."

Delighted with Nita's information, Fitz grabbed her hands across the table. Not the normal response to a police report. She was a bit startled, but not unpleasantly. He quickly withdrew and cleared his throat. "Excellent work, Officer Diaz. Did Raul say what the deal was? Did he name the sailor and his ship?"

"Unfortunately, no. Detective Morales is going to bring him in for questioning. He knows these boys real well, used to run with a gang just like them when he was young and stupid. Now he's a smart old fox. I'll find out if he's got anything yet." She slid out of the booth and went to the pay phone in back.

Fitz took a swallow of beer, and a deep breath. He was grateful for Nita's absence, it gave him time to clear his head. Once his official report was filed, his part in this phase of the investigation would be finished, and as soon as

Nita filed her report, hers would be, too. The detective branch would take over, and they'd both be back on routine patrol. More than six miles separated their precincts. Their paths weren't going to cross by chance. Unlikely that another case would bring them together.

He was weighing his options when Nita returned to the booth. "Raul's still on the loose," she told him. "Joey must have heard that he was shooting his mouth off and told him to make himself scarce. Morales will find him tomorrow."

She looked at her watch. It was after 9:00. "Well, I guess I should be going. My mother will be waiting dinner."

Fitz treated her to his most engaging smile. "Could you call her, tell her not to wait? I was hoping you'd stay and have a bite with me."

"Won't your folks be expecting you?"

"I can call them. They won't mind. There are plenty of mouths to feed at our table, one less won't be missed. Besides, they've probably eaten already."

Nita considered. "We don't have a telephone. I'll have to call the landlady. If she's in, it's a date." They went to the pay phone together.

THIRTY-SIX.

The three men seated at the round table paid no attention to the young couple as they made their way to the back of the bar. They weren't even paying much attention to their drinks, a real novelty. As usual, Harold Rosenberg had the floor.

"You know what I think of the Surrealists' crackpot theories, but that doesn't mean I don't like some of them personally. Not Dalí, of course, he of the ridiculous moustache, he's little more than a clown. Not to mention a publicity hound and a sellout. The man has no shame, designing department store windows and fun-house pavilions and calling them manifestations of his paranoid-critical method, whatever that is. Nothing but hokum, available on order to the highest bidder. Wasn't it Breton who coined his anagram, 'Avida Dollars'? That's right on the money, if you'll forgive the pun." His own cleverness brought a smile to his lips.

"Bill Hayter's okay," he continued. "Peel away the Surrealist veneer and underneath is an English gentleman. He doesn't babble incomprehensible poetry or drone on about the beauty of the marvelous. That printmaking workshop of his is turning out some interesting stuff, and he's a solid craftsman, regardless of the imagery he dreams up. And I've always thought well of Duchamp, as a person

107

if not as an artist, and anyway I don't consider him a Surrealist. He never kowtowed to Breton, far too independent. That's why Breton respects him."

"Vat about Matta?" asked de Kooning. "He don't swallow Breton hook, line, and sinker." A connoisseur of American slang, he never missed an opportunity to use it.

"He thinks he's going to take over." replied Rosenberg. "He's got Breton on the defensive. I was surprised he even showed up at Matta's, especially since Jacqueline was there with David. When I saw her come in on her own I figured she'd had another showdown with her husband. Of course Hare was already there, all the more reason for Breton to stay away. He's stuck with that young upstart as the backer of *VVV*, thanks to which Jacqueline is dumping him, but he doesn't have to socialize with him. So why did he come at all, then just collect Duchamp, and leave?"

"I found out why from the detective who questioned me. Collins was his name," said Motherwell. "Breton needed someone to translate for him when he reported Lam's death. He's the one who found the body."

"So that's why he was in and out in such a rush. How much did Collins tell you, Bob?" Rosenberg wanted to know.

"Almost nothing at first." Motherwell replied. "He said he was looking into an incident involving one of my associates."

"That's what he told me," interrupted Rosenberg. "And me." echoed de Kooning.

"He wanted to know where I was yesterday," Motherwell continued. "I told him I was in the studio working on my collage for Peggy's show. As you know, Maria and I never got to the party. She finds these gatherings tiresome, and I was making good progress, so we decided to stay home. I took a break for supper and went back to work.

"Then he asked if I know Lam. I said, 'Certainly I do, he's a friend, and a damned fine artist.' The word he'd used, 'incident,' came back to my mind. 'Has something happened to him?' I asked. When he told me Lam was dead, my first thought was that he'd been in some kind of accident, but then why question my whereabouts? I confess I was confused, and rather apprehensive, and of course upset." The memory made him reach for his glass and take a healthy swallow.

"I wanted details, and he was quite reluctant to give them. That must be pretty standard, but I argued that I couldn't help him without more to go on. I think he realized I had nothing to do with it, so he told me a few things. Breton went to call for Lam last night and found him on the studio floor. They're treating it as a suspicious death, cause unknown at present, but not an accident or a stroke. In other words, someone killed him, though Collins didn't say as much. No other conclusion to draw, is there?"

Nods from his tablemates.

Motherwell leaned his head on his hand. "Lam, of all people. Whatever ideological differences any of them had with one another, no one ever had a bad word for him. It sounds corny to say it, but he was pure. Oh, he listened to the rhetoric, and even went along with the idea of creativity as a product of the unconscious, but his art came from another place. I've never met anyone for whom it was so genuinely spiritual. If Surrealism helped him reach deeper into the source of his inspiration then, yes, he was a Surrealist, but I think it came naturally to him. Breton and his theories just validated what he was already aiming for."

"Ja," agreed de Kooning, "he vas a natural. I vas nuts about de guy." Yielding to sentiment, he sighed heavily and polished off his whiskey.

THIRTY-SEVEN.

"I'm going to ride uptown with you," Fitz announced as they left the Cedar Tavern. By the time they had finished dinner, lingering over coffee and swapping stories of their exploits in law enforcement, it was after 11:00. Nita protested that she'd be fine going home alone. "Just because I'm not in uniform doesn't mean I can't take care of myself," she told him.

Fitz insisted. "My mother would never let me hear the end of it. And she'd be right. 'A gentleman sees a lady to her door,' she'd say."

"Do you tell your mother everything?" Nita teased.

"I want to tell her about you," he explained, looking at her earnestly. "I'd like her to know that I had dinner with a lovely lady who just happens to be a cop, who I'm sure can take very good care of herself, but who I'd like to be with for a bit longer this evening."

Nita was touched. She slipped her arm through his as they walked to the subway. "You know," she mused, "I think I'd like that, too." She stopped and pulled a serious look. "But we're riding Dutch, understood?" She fished a nickel out of her purse and flashed it at him.

A wide grin spread over Fitz's face. What a corker she is! "Deal," he exclaimed, and shook her free hand vigorously. Their laughter followed them all the way to the IRT station.

At that late hour, the wait between trains was a lot longer, which bothered the couple not at all. What had begun as a business meeting had turned into a social occasion, and Fitz was determined to make it last as long as possible. But the case was still on his mind.

"Tell me something," he asked Nita. "How old is Joey?"

"I'd say about twenty-four, maybe twenty-five. Why do you ask?"

"I suppose his gang are all about the same age, too, or younger," he replied. "I was wondering why they haven't been drafted. You don't see a lot of young, healthy guys around these days who aren't in uniform." He chuckled. "Like me, for instance. I've already got a uniform, which is why I'm not in the Pacific with your brother or with my cousin Liam in Italy. My little brother, Andy. I think his number's coming up soon. But those hoodlums, they're still in civvies. How's that?"

"Believe it or not," Nita explained, "Joey has a legitimate excuse. Asthma. He got a medical deferment because of it. When he went to get the doctor's note, he persuaded the doc to write excuses for his gang members. When I say 'persuaded,' I mean he either bribed him or threatened him. How else do strapping guys like Manuel and Felipe, his two musclemen, get to be 4-F? Manuel suddenly developed a weak heart, though the only weak part of his body is between his ears, and Felipe's newfound hernia doesn't prevent him from lifting crates of stolen liquor. Joey's whole crew got out on medical grounds. Everybody knows they're perfectly fit for service, but nobody would dare squeal to the draft board."

"So while the honest guys march off to war, the crooks do their dirty business as usual," said Fitz, disgusted. If he hadn't been with a woman he would have

111

spat on the subway platform, in spite of the signs saying it was prohibited. "Boy, that gets my Irish up!"

"How do you think I feel," countered Nita, "with my brother overseas while Joey and company piss on the home front? Pardon my French."

That gave Fitz an opening to change the subject. "So you speak French, too. A girl of many talents."

"Watch out who you call a girl, buddy boy, or you'll hear some more of my French and maybe some spicy Spanish to boot."

Fitz gasped, covered his ears, and pulled a shocked expression that gave Nita the giggles.

THIRTY-EIGHT.

When Carlos returned to the *Princesa*, the purser was waiting for him. "I have a message for you," he said, handing him the note.

His first thought was that Joey had further instructions for him, perhaps the name of the contact for the next handoff. Instead it was from Lam's friend Matta. "I must see you urgently," he had written in Spanish. "Come to my place as soon as you get this note." Carlos recognized the address. He had been there before, only a short walk from Lam's. Probably wants to tell me what I already know. Maybe he knows about the deal and wants to warn me. Too late for that. I should just stay on board, forget about Matta, forget about Lam, and lie low.

He folded the note and shoved it in his pocket, where his hand encountered Joey's nine fifties. Better stash them while the rest of the crew are ashore.

With the cash safely tucked away in his hidey-hole, Carlos went on deck for a smoke. The purser joined him at the railing, and Carlos offered him one of his Camels.

His shipmate thanked him and lit up. "Aren't you going to your friend's place?" he asked. "He seemed pretty anxious to see you." Of course he had read the note.

"Oh, sure," replied Carlos. "I just wanted to drop off my ditty bag. I'll see you later." Reluctantly, he crossed the deck and headed down the gangway.

It was not a long walk. Across Gansevoort four blocks to West 4th Street, then eight blocks south to where it crossed West 10th Street, an odd anomaly of numbering in that unconventional neighborhood. From there it was less than two blocks to Lam's place and only one more to Matta's. He took it slow, giving himself time to consider the consequences of what he had done.

When he saw the body crumpled on the studio floor, his first impulse had been to run, but a little voice told him to stop and think. Lam must have been robbed. Someone found out he had the three hundred he was going to pay me, came up here, slugged him when his back was turned, and took it. So now I'm stuck with the dope and no money. I could leave the dope here, but then I get nothing for the risk I took. And if I leave it, and the cops somehow trace it to me, they'll think I killed him. But why would I do that if the deal went through as planned?

Maybe it didn't. Maybe he shorted me and I got sore. Shit, they could probably make that stick, it's only my word. They wouldn't bother looking for anyone else.

He had sat down at the kitchen table, careful not to touch the surface, though he realized that his fingerprints must be all over the apartment from his previous visits. He tried to calm himself, to think straight, but the more he thought the more frightened he got. Lam's friends had seen them together, they'd tell the cops who to look for.

Then his head cleared and he realized that he could make them look in a different direction, toward those weird Surrealists Lam hung out with. He got up from the table and returned to the studio as a picture formed in his mind's eye.

Finding the right props was easy. The rubber chicken's foot was standing behind Lam's easel, where he had placed it so he could sketch its shape on the canvas he was painting. The African mask was hung on the wall nearby, also in position for study. The umbrella was leaning beside the kitchen door with the galoshes. Gingerly, he removed Lam's shoes and socks, and stretched his body out on its back.

When he touched his friend's cool, dark skin, he felt sadness sweep over him. If only he had arrived earlier. Then the voice of common sense urged, work fast and get the hell out before someone finds you. He pulled the socks over his hands and wiped his prints off the shoes. Then he collected the props and created a three-dimensional full-size version of one of the grotesque figures he and Lam had drawn on paper.

When the exquisite corpse was complete, Carlos had put Lam's shoes and socks in the bedroom. Taking up his ditty bag, still containing the undelivered package of cocaine, he hesitated at the studio door and contemplated his handiwork. It must have been one of those crazy artists, he reasoned, so this isn't such a dirty trick. The door was open, after all. Better leave it that way. He let the killer in. Yes, it must have been a fellow Surrealist.

Now, approaching Patchin Place, Carlos reminded himself that Matta is one of them. But surely not the one who robbed and killed him. If he had done it, he wouldn't bother with me. The body must have been discovered, and he probably wants to break the news to me. Warn me not to go near Lam's apartment. I appreciate that.

115

THIRTY-NINE.

Anne Matta was surprised to find a stranger, and a somewhat disreputable looking one at that, standing outside her apartment door. Shifting uneasily from one foot to another, clutching his watch cap in both hands, Carlos eyed her sheepishly.

"Buenas noches, señora. Yo soy Carlos. ¿Está Señor Matta aquí?" he asked, glancing past her, scanning the room.

He had been there once before, with Lam. Over coffee in the studio, Matta had talked about growing up in Chile, and his early training as an architect. His desire to see the world had prompted him to become a Merchant Marine—he and Carlos had that in common. But life at sea was not for him. "Much too hard work," he confessed with charming self-deprecation. Still, it took him to Europe, where he soon fell in with the leading architects and artists of the day. Carlos had never heard of any of them, but Lam said that they were important people.

The ambitious young man had proven himself to be remarkably adaptable, learning French in Paris and English in London. Soon he was working on building projects as far afield as Finland and the Soviet Union. But his base was Paris, where he met Dalí, who in turn introduced him to Duchamp and Breton. For an adventurous fellow like himself. the intellectual, political, and artistic turmoil of those prewar years was magnetic.

With Breton's encouragement, he abandoned architecture, which produced solid, tangible things, and jumped into the void, so to speak. "In Surrealism," he explained, "you have no structure, nothing to grab hold of, nothing to fall back on but your own imagination. That's why I call my paintings 'inscapes.' They show what's inside my head, inside my heart, inside my very soul."

Carlos was not a deeply religious man, but he thought this seemed a bit blasphemous. The idea that serious art should illustrate, not the holy word of God but the base feelings of man, was troubling. In his experience, art had always been a servant of the church, like the opulent carvings and colorful paintings in Cartagena's Catedral Basílica Metropolitana de Santa Catalina de Alejandría, where he sometimes went to pray for safe passage through treacherous waters.

The funny drawings he and Lam made together were just a game, a pastime, not serious. He didn't understand the arcane symbolism or the significance of the hybrid creatures in Lam's paintings, but he knew they had a spiritual dimension that was meaningful to Lam, if not to him.

When he timidly questioned Matta's motives, the artist had laughed out loud. "Haven't you heard," he sneered, "God died on the 17th of July, 1936, the day Spain declared war on herself. Go stare into the empty eyes of the survivors in Guernica and tell them to look to heaven for salvation. As we sit here debating the proper function of art, bombs are raining from the sky onto Europe's cathedrals."

He had checked himself before he became too strident. "You're entitled to your beliefs," he concluded, "just as I'm entitled to mine. I choose to believe in myself."

117

FORTY.

Carlos was recalling this exchange as Anne regarded him coldly. Her Spanish was limited to a few pleasantries, and she had no intention of trying to converse with this unwelcome caller. "Go away," she said.

Anne had been out when Carlos first visited, so she had never seen him before, but she recognized his name. He was part of the scheme her husband, Lam and Hare had cooked up. She wasn't supposed to know anything about it, but she had overheard them planning.

Back in August, on an especially hot afternoon, she had climbed out the bedroom window onto the fire escape to cool off while keeping an eye on the twins, sprawled naked on the bed. Only recently liberated from the damp warmth of her womb, they didn't seem to mind the heat—in fact, they appeared quite comfortable, while she was suffocating in the unventilated room.

As she stood outside the open window, she heard the three artists talking in the studio. That window was also open, and they had no idea she was out there. At first she paid no attention to them, her mind on how pleasant it would be to go up to Darien for the rest of the summer, how tempting to just pack up and quit the city until after Labor Day. If only she could persuade Roberto, though that was unlikely. He was far too proud to subject himself to her parents' unspoken but evident disapproval for any length of time.

Even a weekend was an ordeal for both couples, an exercise in restraint, which, aggravated by her pregnancy, left her tense and moody. But now there were the twins to consider as well, and coping with two infants in this heat was equally exhausting. Perhaps Roberto would let her take the boys on her own. He could manage by himself for a couple of weeks, just until the weather broke.

Her thoughts were interrupted by Hare's voice, saying something about money. He spoke no Spanish, so they had to converse in English.

"We need to figure out the initial cost. I'll put up the stake," he offered, "if you two can work out the other ends."

"My old friends in the Merchant Marine will put me in touch with the right people in South America," said Matta. "Cocaine is flooding out of Peru, all spoken for by the medical corps, but it shouldn't be hard to arrange for a little diversion. I'll find out how much it costs down there. There's probably already a pipeline we can tap into."

"If we can get the goods to Cartagena, I'm sure Carlos can handle the transport," said Lam. "He's an experienced smuggler."

"Okay, let's say we get the stuff to New York. Who buys it from us?" Hare wanted to know.

"I can sell it in Chinatown," Lam told him. "I know who to go to. You give me the money for Carlos to buy it and to pay him when he delivers. Then I sell it and pay you back, with interest. Out of the profit, I give him enough for another run, and Matta and I split what's left."

"Forget the interest," said Hare, "I don't want any of the profits. I'm just putting up the stake so you two can have a steady income. I'm out of it as soon as you get the deals working at both ends. All right, let's investigate this, see if it's feasible. It's up to you, Matta. You find out about supply. and then, if that can work. Lam will find out about demand."

Anne was aghast. Her husband was actually planning a crime! Three crimes, in fact. Stealing cocaine from the army, smuggling it into the country, and selling it to a drug dealer. She almost jumped through the open window into the studio and confronted him. But she hesitated.

He'll think I was deliberately spying on them. she told herself, and anyway they can't possibly go through with it. It's too outlandish. Of course Roberto wants to make money so he doesn't have to take support from my family, but he won't really go that far.

The whole idea is—well, it's surreal.

FORTY-ONE.

Before Anne could close the door on Carlos, her husband appeared behind her. Ever since leaving the note, he had been anxiously awaiting this visit.

"Let him in," he demanded, pulling the door out of her hand. No apology or explanation for his rude behavior. Carlos edged into the room, trying to avoid Anne's angry look. She turned it on her husband. "I don't want him here," she hissed.

Ignoring her, Matta hustled Carlos toward the studio. "We have business," he said over his shoulder. "It won't take long." They went inside and closed the door.

Back in early September, when the aerogram arrived, she had begun to fear that his reckless dream—her nightmare—was becoming a reality. He sometimes received air letters from his relatives in Chile, but this one bore a Peruvian stamp and was postmarked Lima. Unfortunately, he was with her when she picked up the mail from the hall. He was expecting it and quickly snatched it away. He said it was from a cousin, someone he hadn't heard from in a long time and had been worried about. She didn't challenge his lie, but dared to hope the letter told him the plan wouldn't work, that the drugs were not available, so he should forget the idea.

121

Three weeks later, another aerogram came, this time from Colombia. Anne happened to be returning from the store when the postman arrived or she wouldn't have seen it, because her husband was waiting by the door. The postman was nearly at their building when she caught up to him.

"Anything for us?" she had asked him, and he said "Yes, one for your husband, from overseas." "I'll take it," she said, and reached for the envelope. Matta saw them, and called out, "Let me have it, it's addressed to me, isn't it?" He took the letter and disappeared upstairs.

But she had seen the stamp and the postmark, and remembered what they had said about getting the goods to Cartagena—isn't that in Colombia, where this Carlos person would handle the transport? So it was going ahead after all.

FORTY-TWO.

No sooner had the studio door closed behind them than Matta grabbed Carlos roughly by the arm. His expression was as fierce as his grip, and the sailor flinched, more startled than hurt. He had expected sympathetic concern, not manhandling.

"What have you done?" hissed Matta.

Now Carlos was frightened. *My God, he thinks I killed Lam!*

"Please, sir, let me explain," he whispered, not wanting the woman to overhear and not knowing that she didn't understand Spanish. "I did not kill your friend. I went to his place, like I always do when I am in port, and found him dead on the floor. I swear it by Holy Mother Mary."

How much should I tell him, Carlos asked himself. *Just enough so he'll know I had no reason to hurt Lam.* "I would never do such a thing," he continued. "He was good to me, and he was going to help me. We had some business together."

Matta grunted. "I know all about your business deal. Who do you think arranged the delivery in Cartagena? I made a drawing of you and sent it to the contact so he would know you by sight." He grabbed Carlos's other arm and shook him roughly. "Where is the stuff?"

123

Carlos was astonished. Why hadn't he realized that Lam wasn't in this alone? Of course not. Where would he get the front money? He was usually broke, or close to it.

"Please," he begged, "let me go. I will tell you everything, I mean everything I know." Matta relaxed his grip and Carlos sank into one of the easy chairs. The artist planted himself squarely in front of him, crossed his arms, and scowled down at him. "Let me hear it."

"The ship was delayed in Cartagena by a storm," he began. "I had no way to let Lam know that I would be arriving a day late. It was after nine on Saturday when I finally got there, and he was dead. I thought someone had killed him and stolen the payment. I did not know what else to think, and I was afraid someone would tie us together and I would be blamed. So I made the diversion, to point away from me."

"What are you talking about?" asked Matta. "What diversion?"

"The costume," Carlos explained, "to make him look like a Surrealist drawing. You know, an exquisite corpse." He described the embellishments—the mask, the umbrella, the galosh, the chicken foot.

"Jesus fucking Christ, you did what?" Matta lunged at him and gripped his arms again, pulling him up from the chair. Although Carlos was the shorter man, his years at sea had toughened him and made him strong. If he had fought back he could have overpowered Matta, but he was weakened by guilt and overwhelmed by the artist's anger.

Matta pulled the sailor's face close to his. Through clenched teeth, he hissed, "You mean to tell me you tried to incriminate one of us? You little prick!" Disgusted, he pushed Carlos back down in the chair. "No wonder the cop came here looking for clues. Now it makes sense. He did not think it was someone who just broke in. He thought someone who knew Lam killed him."

Matta backed off and began to pace the room. Carlos sank back into the chair, held his breath, and grew tense again as the artist turned on him.

"So you assumed someone had taken the money. You had no idea who—it could have been a total stranger—but you tried to pin it on one of the people who went through hell with him. We thought we had found safe haven here. Thanks to you, we are all under suspicion, just like in Europe." He gritted his teeth. "All except you, that is."

In two steps, Matta was back in Carlos's face. He cringed as the artist confronted him. "How do I know it was not you? I have only your word for it. Suppose you killed him for the money and kept the dope?"

Matta stood up. "By the way, where is the dope? I do not suppose you delivered it to a dead man."

Now Carlos had more explaining to do.

FORTY-THREE.

Even though she couldn't understand more than a few words of their animated Spanish, Anne stood by the closed door and listened as closely as she could to the conversation in the studio. More like a confrontation. She heard Lam's name and the words *Cartagena* and *muerto*. She heard Matta's furious outburst. Maybe the deal was dead after all. Of course Matta would be upset, but what a relief it would be to her!

After she learned that they were going through with the crazy plan, Anne had been trying to think of some way to stop them. She couldn't prevent the smuggling part of it, but once the drugs were in the country maybe she could keep them from going any farther. From what she had overheard in August, Lam was going to handle the sale. If she could find out how much money was involved, she might be able to make a deal with him. She would have to confront him, find out how much it cost, and offer to pay it.

The price of cocaine was a mystery to her, but she was sure it would be several hundred dollars or it wouldn't have been worth the effort and the risk. She would have to get it from her parents. On what pretext could she ask for that kind of money? She certainly couldn't tell them the truth. If she said one of the twins needed medical treatment, they would insist on taking him to the doctor in Darien, or to one of the New York hospitals. It would be the same if she said she was sick herself.

Maybe I could tell them that Roberto has a commission and needs extra money for art materials. He'll pay them back when he gets paid. Then the commission will fall through. That might work. I'll figure out the details later, she reasoned. The important thing, the only thing, is to keep Roberto from becoming a drug dealer.

On the Tuesday after Columbus Day, Matta had suggested to Anne that she take the twins to Darien for a few days, so she guessed that the shipment was due to arrive. She bought a paper, checked the shipping news, and found a listing for the *Princesa*, bound for New York from Cartagena, via Mariel, due in port on the evening of Friday the fifteenth. Since Matta had arranged the South American contact, Anne assumed the drugs would be delivered to him that night or early the next morning. Then he'd pass them along to Lam. Her husband wanted her out of the way while the deal went down. She telephoned her parents and made the arrangements.

Bill Clark had driven down to pick them up on Thursday, happy at the prospect of having them visit without Matta, who had made some excuse about being absorbed in his work and needing to concentrate without distractions. Ordinarily, this might have offended Anne, but it fit right into her cock-and-bull story about the commission, so she played along. His lie made her lie all the more plausible.

During their leisurely drive along Route 1, she hinted to her father that Roberto was working on a major project. She mentioned that Peggy Guggenheim had recently commissioned Jackson Pollock to paint an enormous mural for the lobby of her town house—which was quite true, unlike her suggestion that something similar was in the offing for Matta.

On Saturday morning, she asked to borrow the car.

"I won't park the twins with you for long," she told her mother. "I just want to spend some time on my own, maybe look in the shops, if you don't mind keeping an eye on them."

Her mother took the bait. "Why don't you go for a drive, Anne? The foliage is so lovely now, and you can find a nice place in the country for lunch. My treat." She found her purse, extracted a ten-dollar bill and pressed it into her daughter's hand. "Take as long as you like. You know I'm happy to have the boys all to myself." She gave Anne a conspiratorial wink. "Give me plenty of time to spoil them."

With kisses all around, Anne took the car keys and headed into Darien. She did not go shopping, or for a pleasant country drive, or to lunch at a charming country inn. She parked at the station and caught the next train to Manhattan. In less than an hour she was in Grand Central Terminal, headed for the downtown subway.

FORTY-FOUR.

After Carlos left, Matta sat in the studio for some time. Not only had the drug deal gone sour, but his friend and partner was dead, and thanks to Carlos he and Hare could both be under suspicion of killing him. Of course there was the possibility that, notwithstanding the false evidence, one of their circle actually was responsible. Who could be so hard up that he would kill Lam to get $300?

Matta went through the list in his mind. Not Breton, he has a job with the VOA. Not Duchamp, he has Peggy. So does Ernst, even if he treats her like dirt. Like Ernst, Tanguy married money—Hare's cousin, Kay Sage, in fact. Tchelitchew has a homo boyfriend to support him. Hayter has his printmaking studio, he can support himself. Dalí, with his commercial clients, is persona non grata, shunned by all the other Surrealists, even Lam. I can rule out Masson, he split from the group long before coming to New York. He got back with us for just one show, "Artists in Exile," at Pierre Matisse's gallery, and then only because it wasn't strictly limited to Surrealists.

Besides none of them being desperate for money, none of them knew anything about the smuggling scheme. Or did they? What if Lam let something slip? No, Matta couldn't see that. Even if he had, they would be likely to wish him good luck.

But what about the Americans? Matta continued speculating. Motherwell has family money, his father's a banker on the West Coast. Gerry Kamrowski has a rich collector, supposed to be a baroness, who buys everything he paints. Bill Baziotes has a wife who works.

Pollock? He's a rum one. Moody, volatile, certainly capable of violence. He's been here for group discussions a few times, even played exquisite corpse once or twice. Sympathetic to my ideas about working from the inside out, and he has interesting things to say about Jungian concepts, picked up from that psychiatrist he went to a few years back, even though you have to get a couple of drinks into him before he'll open his mouth.

But a couple more drinks, and he's ready to explode at the least provocation. Lee has to watch him like a hawk, especially now that he's getting ready for his first solo show at Peggy's.

Oh, wait—he has a contract with Peggy. "My new genius," she calls him. He's getting a regular paycheck from her, plus extra cash to buy the materials for her mural. If I had a sweet deal like that, I wouldn't need to smuggle cocaine.

Matta's head was beginning to swim again. He realized he hadn't eaten since Anne fixed him a late breakfast. But he needed to let Hare know what Carlos had told him. They had to cut him loose, he was getting a much better deal uptown, and Lam was the connection to the Chinatown buyer, so they had no way to pass the stuff along even if Carlos could be persuaded to continue supplying.

Besides, they had no leverage. They couldn't threaten to finger him because if they did, he would implicate them. Hare would go to jail and I'd get deported, Matta realized. And if Carlos is telling the truth, we still don't know who actually killed Lam. One of us could be charged with his murder.

What a nightmare, worse than the most bizarre Surrealist fantasy.

FORTY-FIVE.

Anne had retreated to the bedroom when she heard Carlos leaving. He and Roberto were still talking heatedly in Spanish, Carlos eager to escape and Matta apparently furious. "¡Vete al diablo!" he had hissed as Carlos bolted for the exit. Then her husband slammed the door behind him, stamped back to the studio, and slammed that door. She decided to let him cool off.

Fortunately he hadn't agitated the twins, who were awake and ready for their evening feeding. She would go to the kitchen and take care of that chore while Roberto calmed down. She had both bottles going when she heard him emerge from the studio and leave the apartment without a word to her.

Once on the street, Matta headed for the nearest phone booth. Hare was waiting for his call.

"Did you find Carlos?"

"I left the note at his ship, like we agreed, and he came to my place. He just left. Wait until you hear his story."

Matta unloaded the whole sorry tale on Hare, who listened with hardly an interruption. More than one dime was inserted into the coin slot before the story was finished.

"He said he found Lam dead. He said he didn't take the money. Do you believe him?" asked Hare.

132

"I don't know what to think," Matta replied. "If he killed Lam, why would he come to see me? My guess is that he thought I wanted to tell him his friend was dead, give him a warning to steer clear. From his reaction, he had no idea I was involved in the deal until I told him. He probably took the money, but there'd be no point in leaving the package, whether or not he killed Lam. So he found another buyer."

"There's only one way it makes sense," reasoned Hare. "Solana already had the uptown deal lined up. He knows there's three hundred waiting for him at Lam's, so he goes there, knocks Lam out, and takes the cash. He doesn't mean to kill him, just double cross him, but he hits him too hard. When he sees what he's done, he thinks quick and dresses up the body to throw the cops off. Then he heads up to Harlem and sells the dope for more than what we offered. He gets paid twice, and the cops are looking for one of us instead of him, the double-dealing son of a bitch."

"You're forgetting something," Matta pointed out. "How did he know what an exquisite corpse looks like?"

Hare had the answer. "From hanging around with Lam, of course. Don't you remember, he was at Breton's once when we played the game? He didn't participate, but he watched."

"So you think Solana is the killer?"

"Who else could it be?"

Matta was still skeptical. "That doesn't explain why he answered my note. If he did it, he'd want to stay as far away from Lam's friends as possible."

Hare had another thought. "What time did he say he found the body?"

"Around nine o'clock last night. The ship was held up by a storm, he said. Didn't make port until Saturday evening. That's why he didn't deliver on Friday as planned."

"I'm going to talk to Breton, see if he knows what time Lam was killed. Also find out when Solana's ship actually arrived. If Lam was dead before the ship docked, Solana's off the hook for the killing."

"Then somebody else will be on the hook," Matta reminded him.

FORTY-SIX.

It was late when Hare got to Breton's apartment, and Jacqueline hushed him as he entered. She threw her arms around his neck and tipped her head back for a kiss, but he did not respond. Realizing he was preoccupied, she withdrew.

"Aube is asleep in the front room," she told him. "She has school tomorrow. André is in the bedroom, working on a poem. Lam's death was such a shock. He's trying to use that feeling in a positive way, to turn it into something creative. He's been wrestling with it ever since he woke up, except when the policeman came to question me."

"I must see him, Jacqueline. I have to ask him something important. Please translate for me."

"Of course," she said, and led him to the bedroom door. Knocking gently, she opened it to reveal Breton seated at a small desk, his head in his hands, staring at a blank sheet of paper. Several pages covered in his small, precise handwriting were scattered on the floor.

"David et ici, mon cher," she began. "He says it is urgent that he speak to you."

"Bonsoir, André," said Hare, exhausting his French.

Breton looked haggard. "What time is it?" he asked. When Jacqueline told him the hour, he groaned. "I must be

135

at the studio at 5:00 a.m. to broadcast live," he said with a sigh. "I must rest, perhaps I can sleep for a few hours."

"I will only be a moment," Hare promised, which Breton understood without the need of translation.

He sat on the bed with Jacqueline beside him— not too close, for propriety's sake, though Breton was well aware of their relationship—and asked his question.

"Do you know what time Lam died?"

"I could not tell precisely. I found him at around half past ten, perhaps a bit later, and he had not been dead for long. There was no rigor mortis," a term Hare recognized, "but when I returned with Duchamp at eleven it was beginning to set in, so I would say that he died around eight in the evening. But that is only a guess."

"Could it have been later, after nine?"

"I doubt it," said Breton. "Under normal conditions, rigor begins about three hours after death. The body was quite cool, and the apartment was a comfortable temperature. It was not a hot night, so rigor would not have been accelerated."

Hare absorbed this information in silence. Then he rose, thanked Breton, and turned to leave.

"Un moment, je t'en prie," said Breton. "May I ask why you wish to know the time of death?"

Hare glanced at Jacqueline as she translated. He would not be able to confirm the time of the *Princesa*'s arrival until Monday morning.

"I spoke to Duchamp," he lied. "He told me about the exquisite corpse costume on the body. It points to a Surrealist as the killer. I have a different idea, but I have to put the pieces together. The time of death is one piece. When I have the other, I will answer your question."

Monday morning, October 18

FORTY-SEVEN.

Detective Hector Morales was a big man in several respects. He was six foot three, barrel-chested, beefy without being overweight. His gravelly baritone made a big impression when he questioned suspects, and when he reassured crime victims that he would get to the bottom of their cases. He also had a big reputation for doing just that.

Morales had a pretty good idea where Raul was hiding out. The punk had a girlfriend whose widowed mother owned a little bodega on 103rd Street, and the two women lived over the store. That's probably where he is, reasoned Morales. Joey lets him discount her protection payments, so she can hardly refuse to take him in if he's in trouble. Anyway, it's not real trouble, like if he knifed somebody. Although shooting off his mouth could be a crime in Joey's book. There were no grounds for a search warrant, so he'd have to talk his way in.

He waited until 11:00 a.m., after the morning rush and before the lunchtime crowd, and intercepted Mrs. Gomez as she came out from behind the counter to straighten up the magazine rack. He had known her since he was a juvenile delinquent boosting Hershey Bars and packs of Wrigley's gum while her back was turned. In those days he thought of himself as a master criminal, immune from detection.

It wasn't until much later that he learned she knew exactly what he was doing and had ratted him out to his mother, who always came in and paid for whatever he took. He had a deep respect for them both—hard-working uncomplaining women who held their families together as best they could. When Mrs. Gomez's husband died and his own father deserted the family, the women just kept on keeping on.

When Hector turned eighteen, his mother had sat him down and had the talk with him. "I know you've been kind of wild," she said, not in a scolding way but matter of fact. She told him about paying for what he took from the bodega, and that she knew he hung out with boys who did worst things, like stealing cars and mugging people. What she didn't say was whether she knew he'd done those things himself a few times. "I smell the marijuana on your clothes," she said, "but I don't mention it because you only smoke it to go along with your friends."

He didn't understand what she was getting at. She wasn't judging him or telling him to stop acting badly. He felt embarrassed that he'd been so inept. And she had covered for him. That made him even more embarrassed. Suddenly he realized this was all wrong. She should have been ashamed of him, behaving like a fool, not caring about the future, letting her down. But she wasn't.

Not in so many words, she was telling him she had faith in him. After all, he had graduated from high school—not dropped out like so many other boys in the neighborhood—and even had decent grades. Luckily none of his petty crimes had attracted the attention of the law. He knew this was a turning point, and it was his decision which way to turn.

Hector Morales had turned right. Right into the Police Academy. As one of the few Hispanic recruits in the

1920s, he was subject to plenty of ribbing, some good-natured, some malicious. But he shrugged it off, didn't blow his top like a dumb street hoodlum with a hair trigger. That was the old Hector, the one he was determined to leave behind.

To his friends' astonishment and his mother's delight, he took to policing as if he had been born on the force. He never slacked off, never took favors or gave them, and earned a reputation for honesty. Even after the introduction of a new cleaning product prompted the nickname Spic and Span, he didn't take offense. Instead he joked that he was the only clean officer in the 23rd.

After five years as a patrolman, he put in for detective and won promotion on the first try. Now, at age thirty-three, he had perfected the art of investigative policing. Behind his back, they now called him el zorro, the fox. He knew it, and was proud of it.

He towered over Mrs. Gomez, but made no effort to intimidate her. Instead he leaned down and embraced her warmly, planting a kiss on each of her plump cheeks. Usually she would reciprocate, but not this time. Her uneasiness told him that he had guessed correctly.

"I know he is here, little mother," he said in Spanish. "I need to talk to him. I don't have a warrant, but tell him I do so he won't blame you for letting me in."

Her distress was evident. "I had to take him. He said Joey wanted him out of the way for a while. Just a couple of days. How could I say no?"

The question was rhetorical. "Of course you could not," Morales replied. "Your Gloria is foolish to run around with a loser like Raul, but she does, so you are stuck with him." He smiled understandingly, and Mrs. Gomez grimaced.

"He is a pig," she said. "Does not lift a finger, expects us to wait on him. He has only been here since

139

yesterday evening, and Gloria is as sick of him as I am. I wish you did have a warrant."

"Once I'm in," the detective explained. "I do not need a warrant to arrest him if he withholds evidence in connection with a crime, and I have reason to believe he will. Or at least try to, until I persuade him otherwise."

FORTY-EIGHT.

Detective Morales followed Mrs. Gomez up the back stairs that led from the office to the apartment above the bodega. First he had asked her to lock the street entrance and back door in case his target made a run for it. He knew the apartment layout and figured he could corner Raul before he caught on, but why take a chance? Mrs. Gomez said he had set himself up in the living room.

"The lazy bum is probably on the couch. No way would I give him my bed, and he is certainly not sleeping with my Gloria," she insisted. "She is a good girl."

"Is she here?" he asked.

"No, she is at work. She works at the Cosmo Theater two days a week, in the box office. She wants to help out, more than just in the shop. To bring in some money, you know. Such a good girl. Not like that boyfriend of hers. Never offered a penny to pay for his food." She made a noise that indicated just what she thought of him.

They climbed the stairs in silence. When they reached the second floor, Morales motioned to Mrs. Gomez to walk ahead of him. Her heels clicked on the bare wood, a sound Raul recognized. He was sitting on the couch, playing solitaire on the coffee table.

"Hey, mama," he bellowed, without looking up. "I'm dying of thirst, bring me a beer."

His only manners are bad ones, said Morales to himself. I'll teach the little jerk some respect. He moved out from behind Mrs. Gomez, who retreated to the kitchen, and was blocking the exit before Raul realized who he was.

"You want a beer, you can get it yourself," he said, "but not before we have a little talk."

For a moment Raul was too startled to reply. He had crossed paths with the detective more than once, but his main contact with the law was a nod to the beat cops who looked the other way when he made his collections. He quickly tried to mask his surprise with a smirk.

"Well, if it ain't Spic and Span. Nice of you to drop in." He rose from the sofa. "I was just leaving."

Morales was on him before he was fully upright.

"Don't be in a hurry, Raul. It's not polite." A firm hand eased the young man back onto the seat.

Raul was indignant. "You can't push me around, cop. I ain't done nothing."

Morales loomed over him. "I heard different."

The smirk was back. "You're blowing smoke, Morales." He started to rise again.

The detective's hand shot out and grabbed Raul's shirt, dragging him up to standing but keeping him slightly off balance. It happened so quickly that Raul was caught off guard. Before he could recover, Morales pulled him close and spoke very softly. He found this tactic far more effective than shouting.

"We're going to have that conversation now, Raul. And you need to mind your manners. You'll address me as Detective Morales or sir. Otherwise I'll arrange a blue shadow for you. I can make things very hard for you on the street, so hard that Joey will cut you loose. He's already wondering if you're a liability. You know that word?" He tightened his grip a bit.

Raul took a moment to weigh his options. Then he caved. "Yeah, I know it. Sir."

142

"Good. We understand each other." Morales let him loose.

Raul sank down on the couch, smoothing out his bunched shirtfront.

Morales took a chair opposite him. "Let's keep it quiet so we don't disturb Mrs. Gomez," he advised. Now his tone was neutral, neither threatening nor friendly, harder for Raul to read.

"I don't care about the sailor's deal with Joey," he began, taking Raul by surprise again. Not blowing smoke after all. "What I'm interested in is the homicide. Has it occurred to you that the sailor may have been the guy who killed Lam? And if he did, and you're covering for him, you're an accessory to murder."

Saturday morning, October 16

Anne emerged from the subway at Christopher Street and headed east toward Lam's apartment, only a block from her own. She had resolved to confront him, try to bribe him, even threaten him with the police if he didn't give up the smuggling scheme, but she was beginning to have second thoughts. What if Roberto was there? She was keeping an eye out for him on the street, but he might be at Lam's. In that case, she told herself, she would have to confront them both and suffer the consequences.

What if she was too late and Lam was already on his way with the drugs to wherever he was planning to sell them? As she reached his building she squared her shoulders. Only one way to find out.

She rang the bell. It was answered. The latch was released, and she went in.

When she got to Lam's third-floor apartment, the door was open. She paused for a moment, listening for voices, hoping she wouldn't hear Roberto's. It was quiet, so she knocked and called out to Lam.

"Hello, Fredo. It's Anne Matta. I need to speak to you."

Lam stepped out of the studio, a puzzled expression on his face. He was clearly expecting someone else.

"Anne. What a surprise. I thought, ah. . . . " he stammered. She was supposed to be at her parents' place in Connecticut, safely out of the way. He stopped himself, realized he was being rude. "Are you looking for Roberto?"

"No," she said. "I thought he might be here, but I'm relieved that he isn't." She closed the door and advanced toward him.

"I know about the shipment," she began, looking him in the eye, not giving him a chance to interrupt. "What

144

*you are doing is wrong, not just morally. It's criminal, as
I'm sure you know. All three of you could go to jail. Maybe
you and David are willing to risk that, but Roberto has a
family to think of."*

Lam was taken aback. *How could she know? Surely
Matta hadn't told her. Somehow she had found out, and she
was furious. If Carlos showed up now she could cause real
trouble. How to get rid of her? Perhaps he could make her
see reason.*

"*Don't you realize it's the family that he is thinking
of? There's no market for his paintings, not yet anyway,
and how long can he go on sponging off your parents
before he loses all self-respect? This is his chance to make
enough money to support you and the twins."*

"*If he's so desperate to earn money,*" she
countered, "*he can go back to practicing architecture or
work in a defense plant or something else, anything that's
legal.*" She was beginning to seethe. "*You put him up to
this. I heard you planning it in August. At the time I thought
it was just a stupid pipe dream, I never thought you'd go
through with it."*

She gave Lam a hard look. "*When I came in, you
were expecting someone to pick up the drugs, weren't you?
They're here, aren't they? The ship arrived yesterday."*

"*The package never came, Anne. Something went
wrong. The deal is off."*

"*You're lying,*" she shouted, her anger and
frustration building. "*I know it's here. I'll buy it from you.
I can get the money. How much do you want for it?*"

"*Please, Anne, I don't have it,*" he insisted. *That
was not a lie.* "*Besides, where would you get the money?
From your father? I'd like to hear you explain why you
want it."*

She had thought about that on the train ride down
from Darien. Obviously going to her parents was out of the
question.

145

"I'll get it from Peggy. She won't want to see any of her artists mixed up in something like this."

She barged into the studio and began moving around the room, looking for hiding places, with no idea just what she was looking for, what sort of package, how big.

After she had made a thorough search of Lam's apartment, Anne headed back uptown to catch a return train to Darien. It had not taken her long to satisfy herself that the drugs weren't there. The apartment was small—only two rooms and a kitchen—and Lam had little furniture. The studio, with its worktable, easel, and props, offered few places of concealment, though she looked behind the African mask hanging on the wall by the fireplace and behind the tall mirror leaning next to it, and turned the rubber chicken's foot upside down and shook it. Likewise the galoshes in the kitchen, where the cabinet under the sink was also inspected.

When she started to rummage through his things, Lam had tried to stop her. He grabbed her arm as she reached for the mask. "Don't touch that," he cried, "it's magic!"

"So that's where it is," she hissed, and wrenched her arm free, pushing him away with all the strength her anger and desperation could muster. Caught off balance, he stumbled back, tripped on the hearth, and fell, hitting his head on the marble mantelpiece, a remnant of the building's former life as a comfortable town house. With a moan, he crumpled to the floor and lay in a heap at her feet.

Seizing the advantage, Anne continued her search without interference. Her attention called to the fireplace, she peered up the chimney but saw only sooty blackness, no ledge or niche where a package could be stashed. The rest of her efforts proved equally frustrating. In the bedroom, she checked the drawers, the closet, under the pillows on *the bed, under the mattress. When her search turned up nothing, she assumed that she was too late and the drugs were already in Chinatown. By the time she finished, Lam was coming around.*

She had to go. She had been away for nearly two hours, and it would take her another hour to get back to her parents' house. A longer absence would be hard to explain. She couldn't say she'd been for a leisurely drive, since her father would surely notice that there was hardly any more mileage on the odometer. Her only excuse was a quiet morning of window-shopping along Main Street, lunch at the soda fountain, perhaps a walk in Tilly Pond Park or down to the beach at Pear Tree Point.

Once on the train, Anne cursed herself for not having acted sooner. She should have confronted the three of them back in August, when she heard them hatching the scheme. She should have told Roberto that she knew what was going on when the letter arrived from Colombia in September. And now she had missed her opportunity to intercept the shipment. Damn, damn, damn—the words seemed to echo in her head, but it was only the train's pulsing rhythm.

Anne collected her thoughts. No use agonizing over past mistakes. What to do now? Only one thing. Stop it from happening again.

Monday afternoon, October 18

FORTY-NINE.

By the time Ricky Wong rang Yun Gee's buzzer, the artist had made the studio more presentable. After he got back from On Leong, he had focused on the room and was disgusted by its condition. Visiting the tong headquarters had sobered him but good. "My mother would die if she could see me like this," he said out loud. But she was in China, and she hadn't seen him in more than two decades.

He looked again at the canvas that always hung prominently in whatever studio he occupied, the one he called *Where Is My Mother*. He painted it when he was only twenty-one and about to leave San Francisco for Paris, thousands of miles farther away from her. It was the self-portrait of a young man suspended between two worlds, staring out of a fragmented environment where home and family were concepts as abstract as the painting's Cubist structure. The tears that streamed down his cheeks were echoed on his mother's, but he did not comfort her. He had turned his back on that world, and seemed to know he would never return.

He went to work right away. The rest of the day was spent cleaning and tidying until the place was looking orderly, with the floor swept, the dishes washed, the blanket neatly folded on the couch, his clothes put away, and his materials laid out as they should be. That was the way he liked things. Even if they were shabby, they didn't have to be messy, dirty, as if he didn't care. Then he took a sponge bath in the studio slop sink and put on a clean shirt.

Being on his own like this was not good for him. He knew he should go home and make up with Helen, in fact he couldn't even remember what they had quarreled about. When he thought of her and their beautiful baby daughter in the apartment she kept so nice, with the bird cages and his chess board and his art books and musical instruments all arranged just so, he felt very sorry for himself. That was his world now, he reminded himself, and he was lucky to have it.

Then Gee remembered what the fight was about. His drinking. Remorsefully, he emptied the rest of the pint of Four Roses into the sink. He took the bottle and the other empties with him as he left, and dumped them in the trash barrel on the corner. Then he headed home.

When he came back on Monday, it was not to escape from Helen's disapproval. With the resilient optimism of youth—she was only twenty-three to his thirty-seven—she had forgiven him, again. Once more he resolved to stay sober and get to work. He was preparing a new canvas when he heard the buzzer and looked out the studio window to see a young Chinese man standing at the door. He felt a mixture of concern and relief. If On Leong was involved, they wouldn't have sent anyone to tell me, he reasoned. He pressed the latch release.

Ricky Wong was a pimply teenager with bad teeth and a swagger that masked his lack of sophistication. Probably someone's Cantonese relative who's been shipped to America for training, reasoned Gee. He knew the type. He had been born in that region.

Ricky was practicing his rudimentary English. He talked like a joke Chinaman, what the white culture

149

contemptuously called a Charlie. "Bossman senme," he said.

It made Gee wince to hear him, but he swallowed his distaste. *Better to speak Cantonese so I don't have to listen to his pathetic pidgin.* He had no intention of inviting him inside, so he stood in the studio doorway. "You have news for me?" he asked, redundantly. *Why else would the kid be here?*

"On Leong did not do it," Ricky informed him. "Nobody in Chinatown did it."

He probably doesn't even know what he's talking about, thought Gee. "Tell your boss I am grateful to know that we have not been dishonored by one of our own. Can you remember that?"

"Sure," sneered Ricky. *Who was this old drunk to question his intelligence?* They had told him all about Gee, and how he was a stooge for the white cops who were trying to pin Lam's killing on one of the tongs. In fact Lam was no good to On Leong dead. He was going to supply them with a valuable commodity, for which he would be paid $1,000 for every shipment. Of course a rival tong might have got wind of the deal and tried to scotch it, but they'd be more likely to offer Lam a better deal than to kill him. No, Lam's death was Chinatown's loss, and On Leong wanted the cops to know that.

Gee made his way to the drugstore and used the pay phone to call in his report to O'Connell.

FIFTY.

Still baffled by the outfit on the body, Collins decided to revisit Motherwell, the most articulate and forthcoming of the people he had questioned. Not hostile like the Krasner dame, or argumentative like Pollock and that Rosenberg guy, or clueless like de Kooning and the Matters. For an artist, he seemed pretty down to earth. From what Collins had seen in his apartment, his art was nothing but a jumble of shapes and colors. At least it wasn't creepy like Lam's.

Since the Chinatown connection looked like a dead end and the voodoo angle wasn't panning out, reasoned Collins, maybe it had something to do with Lam's art. After all, some of the decorations—the chicken's foot, the mask— were his props. You could see them, distorted versions of them anyway, in the painting he was working on. It was like he was posing for his own picture. I guess they usually hire models, but if he was as poor as everyone says, he couldn't afford one. Yeah, but you can't get yourself up like that after you're dead.

Yet Collins had a hunch it was art-related. He decided to take along the full-body photograph and see what Motherwell made of it. He telephoned and found the artist at home.

151

"This is Detective Collins calling, Mr. Motherwell," he began politely. "I spoke to you on Sunday about Wifredo Lam's death."

"Yes, of course," replied the artist. "Have you learned anything more? Do you know the cause of death?"

"I do have more information, and I think you may be able to help me make sense of it. Is it okay if I come to see you now?"

Motherwell was intrigued, though a bit uneasy. "By all means. West 8th Street, number 33, as you may recall. My name is on the bell."

"I'll be right over," said Collins, and rang off.

It was a short walk, but long enough for Collins to formulate his approach. I think I'll just show him the photo, get his reaction, and take it from there, he decided. No need to go into the Cuban or Chinese angles, unless he brings it up. Don't want to point him in the wrong direction.

Motherwell was waiting for him at the front door. "My wife just came in with a friend," he announced. "They're having coffee in the parlor, so let's go into the studio. We can talk freely there."

He directed the detective to the back of the building, where a bedroom with a north window had been converted into his workspace. On a large easel, a bold abstract painting in progress dominated the room. Several unfinished collages lay on the worktable, and one wall was covered with sketches, postcard reproductions of paintings, magazine clippings, and a photograph of a frowning man.

"Who's the grump?" asked Collins, then excused himself. "Sorry, I hope he's not a relative."

"Charles Baudelaire, a nineteenth-century French poet," replied the artist. "He defined what it means to be modern, and I try to work in his spirit."

Doesn't look like much fun, thought Collins, but then it seems these artists take themselves pretty seriously. He decided not to get into the subject of what motivated

152

Motherwell, way too deep for him. Better get down to business.

Motherwell directed him to a chair that looked like it had been stolen from a sidewalk café. It was the only chair in the room, so Collins politely remained standing. With disarming frankness, he began.

"I don't mind telling you, this case has me stumped. The autopsy report says he died from a blow to the head. Someone hit him from behind. He let the person into the apartment, so he probably knew whoever it was. No sign of a struggle. and as far as we can tell, nothing was taken."

Motherwell found that incredible. "You mean someone he knew attacked him in his own apartment for no apparent reason?"

"Did he have any enemies? Anyone with a score to settle?"

"Of all the people I know," said Motherwell. "Lam is the least likely to have enemies. Excuse me, I mean was. It's still hard for me to accept the fact that he's dead, even harder to believe someone killed him."

"There's more to it," continued Collins, "which is why I need your advice. The body was, well . . . tampered with after death." He pulled out the photograph and laid it on the worktable by the window. "What do you make of that?"

Motherwell stared at the picture of Lam's body. He clearly was taken aback. "Good God," he whispered, "an exquisite corpse."

"Hideous is more like it," said Collins with evident disapproval. It was beyond disrespectful to call that get-up exquisite. unless you have a really warped sense of humor. He scowled at the artist.

"You misunderstand me," replied Motherwell. "I don't mean it literally, except that it is Lam's corpse. I'm sorry, I'm not making myself clear." He sank down on the chair and collected himself.

"Lam belonged to a circle of artists and writers who call themselves the Surrealists," he explained. "Their art is inspired by unconscious impulses, anyway that's the idea. It has to be spontaneous, irrational, beyond ordinary experience. They use certain devices—tricks, if you like—to stimulate their imaginations. One of them is a drawing game they call *le cadavre exquis* in French. In English, that means 'the exquisite corpse.' The name comes from one of their poems, a combination of unrelated words, the more absurd the better.

"It's played in a group. One person starts a figure by drawing the head, then folds that part back so you can't see what was drawn." He took a piece or paper from the worktable and demonstrated. "Then it's handed to the next person, who draws the torso and the arms, folds that part back, and hands it on. The last person finishes it off with legs and feet. Then the paper is unfolded and they see what sort of hybrid they've created."

He unfolded his paper. At the top, he had drawn a mask-like face. In the middle section, one arm sprouted an umbrella and the other ended in a boot. The last section had the figure standing on a clawed foot.

"They always try to make it as bizarre as possible, and that's exactly what someone has done to Lam's body."

Collins compared the drawing to the photograph. He let out a breath that was half whistle, half sigh. "I'll be damned." Suddenly the list of potential suspects came into focus.

Motherwell was also aware of the implication. "I can't imagine one of the Surrealists killing Lam," he insisted. "As I said before, he was admired, even loved, by everyone in the group. Oh, there's plenty of contention in the ranks, but he never took sides. André Breton is the leader, and he can be dictatorial—he decides who's in and who's out. I could see someone wanting to wring *his* neck."

At the mention of Breton, Collins interjected, "I think I told you he's the guy who found Lam's body. Even if they did have a dispute, he's the one Surrealist we can rule out as the killer."

"How do you know?" asked Motherwell.

"Because he was uptown at the Voice of America studio all day on Saturday. He told us that, through his buddy Duchamp, when we questioned him, and we checked his story. He got in around nine in the morning, and didn't leave until 10:00 p.m. According to the autopsy, Lam was clobbered some time that morning, but after eleven, when he went to the candy store on Sixth Avenue for a pack of cigarettes. The guy at the counter saw him there, alive and well."

FIFTY-ONE.

After a productive conversation with Raul, Detective Morales returned to the 23rd Precinct to find Officer Diaz emerging from the squad room.

"Hola. Nita," he called, as she approached. "I have some interesting news from the Joey and Raul front. Come to my office and I'll fill you in."

"So you found that little rat Raul? Of course you did. What hole was he hiding in?"

"Mrs. Gomez's place, over the bodega. Her daughter's his girlfriend, worse luck for her," replied Morales. "They didn't have any choice but to take him in, since he cuts Mrs. G. a deal on protection. He acted tough, tried to bluff his way out, but when I mentioned a possible charge of accessory after the fact to murder, he suddenly got real helpful."

"What was the deal he was bragging about?" asked Nita. "And what's the connection to Lam's killing?"

"I told him I wasn't interested in the deal," Morales explained. "but I'm sure it's a smuggling racket. The sailor, name of Carlos Solana, is off a Colombian ship that makes regular runs to New York via Cuba. Lots of opportunity to pick up all sorts of contraband. Anyway, that angle can wait. The important thing is that Raul found out about Solana while he was on Lam's trail. Raul told me that the deal was originally between Solana and Lam, but when the sailor got to the apartment Lam was dead. So he went looking for another deal."

Like any good investigator, Nita was skeptical. "Do you buy that, Hector? Suppose Solana double-crossed Lam. Maybe he already had a better offer from Joey."

"Then why go to Lam's at all?" reasoned Morales. "Why not just take his stuff straight uptown?"

"He wanted his payoff from Lam," said Nita, "so he went there first. Figured he'd get paid, knock Lam out, and then go uptown."

Morales chuckled. "You bucking for detective? Okay, then, why didn't he take the three hundred bucks Lam had on him?"

"Maybe Lam held out on him, said he didn't have the money yet. Said he had to pass the goods first, then pay Solana. Solana gets sore, they argue, and Solana beans him when he isn't looking. He panics. Realizes he's killed the guy and decides he'd better scram."

Morales recognized the big hole in that scenario.

"Then who dressed him up like a voodoo doll? That must have taken some time—plenty of time to go through his pockets—and some thought. Not the work of a panicky killer."

"No, it isn't," she agreed. "And we don't know why it was done, much less who did it. We'd better find this Carlos Solana."

"His ship is the *Princesa*," Morales told her. "Let's find out where she's docked." He reached for the intercom and buzzed the desk.

"Sergeant, call the Port of New York Authority and get the whereabouts of a freighter now in port, Colombian registry, the *Princesa*. Ring me as soon as you have the information."

While they waited, Morales briefed Nita on the details of his interview with Raul. "He called me Spic and

Span, the little punk. I know I'll never get away from that nickname, though I've learned to shrug it off. But coming out of his mouth, right to my face, it almost got under my skin."

"No one on the force calls you that anymore," she assured him. "They have a much better nickname for you now, you foxy old flatfoot."

Morales grinned as the phone rang. His good mood died when the desk sergeant relayed the bad news. "The *Princesa* was tied up at Pier 52. She left port five hours ago, all hands aboard."

FIFTY-TWO.

Fitz was just leaving the station when the desk sergeant called him to the phone. "It's yer Spanish lady friend at the 23rd on the line," he said with a grin. "I think she fancies ya."

Fitz bristled. "She's a police officer, Sergeant Ryan, just you remember that. She's calling on official business, I'm sure. Give me the phone. Fitzgerald speaking. What is it, Officer Diaz?"

From his abrupt tone, Nita got the message loud and clear. Keep it strictly impersonal. Desk sergeants have sharp ears.

"It's the Lam case, Officer Fitzgerald," she began. "I have good news and bad news." She told him what Morales had learned, and about the unfortunate departure of the ship with Solana aboard.

"I don't know if Pier 52 is where the *Princesa* always docks, but we can find out. Or rather you can, since it's in your jurisdiction. From what Detective Morales tells me, Solana had motive and opportunity. If he returns with the ship, you can pick him up. If he doesn't, it's probably an admission of guilt, but then he's out of reach."

Fitz agreed. "He's not likely to come back if he's the killer, is he? But if he does, we'll be waiting for him, thanks to you and Morales for fingering him. Once he leaves the dock and steps onto West Street, he's ours."

"I'll send you a copy of the written report as soon as it's filed," she told him. Meanwhile he decided to brief Collins and O'Connell right away. It was all over the station house that the commissioner was putting on the pressure, and this information would show that progress was being made.

"Excellent work, Officer Diaz," he said, as flatly as the pleasure of hearing her voice allowed. "I'll pass this information to the detectives on the case. I believe you know Collins. I'm sure he'll want to thank you himself."

He rang off with a curt goodbye, secure in the knowledge that she saw through his formal façade.

FIFTY-THREE.

"Now we're making progress!" thundered O'Connell when Fitz relayed the latest news from the 23rd. "Although it's a shame Morales didn't get hold of his fink last night. We could have collared that sailor this morning before he shipped out. Damn."

His fist hit the desk, but not too hard. Now he had a likely suspect, as well as a good excuse why he couldn't make an immediate arrest. He got on the intercom and ordered a call to the commissioner's office.

When Valentine was put through, O'Connell informed him, "We have a break in the Lam case, sir. A suspect has been identified."

Valentine was momentarily at a loss. "Lam, you say? Oh yes, the artist friend of Peggy's. Funny name. Funny looking, too, now that I recall. Met him once, bit of an oddball. But that's beside the point. What have you got?"

O'Connell filled him in. The complication of Solana's disappearance was accepted as regrettable but not disastrous. "I'll have the Port Authority radio the ship, find out if she's making any stops between here and home port. If they can put the fellow ashore on American soil, the FBI can pick him up."

"I appreciate this information. O'Connell," Valentine declared. "I'm glad I can inform Peggy that my men have identified the killer."

O'Connell hesitated to remind the commissioner that the case against Solana was far from proven, but what harm could it do for him to tell some meddling socialite that the crime had been solved, even if the killer had escaped? It would take the pressure off and Valentine could forget all about Lam.

"I'll let you know right away when there are further developments." O'Connell promised, knowing that Valentine would have no more interest in the case. After being told that he was free to call any time, day or night, the detective rang off in good spirits. We may not have solved the murder, he told himself, but I've solved my problem. He made a note to call and thank Hector Morales.

He buzzed the clerk's office. "Better try to locate Lam's next of kin. Supposed to have a wife and family in Havana. Call the Cuban Consulate, find out if they know anything about them."

FIFTY-FOUR.

Collins returned to the 6th Precinct to find O'Connell in a very good mood indeed. He wasted no time in telling the detective that he'd managed to get Valentine out of his hair.

"I've fingered the prime suspect, Pat," he boasted, then revised his statement. "Thanks to the outstanding work of Morales and Diaz up at the 23rd. They made the connection to Lam. He's a Cuban, all right. Let me give you the details."

Settled in one of O'Connell's office chairs, Collins got the story so far.

"Our big problem is that the guy shipped out before we could collar him. I'm waiting to hear from the Port Authority whether we can get him off the ship before she's out of U.S. waters. Otherwise we can kiss Solana goodbye."

"Just how solid is the case against him, Jack?"

"Well, we know from the uptown information that Solana and Lam had some kind of deal that went sour. Smuggling, most likely. Then there's the Cuban voodoo outfit on the body. We also have a lot of unidentified fingerprints from Lam's place, and if we can match Solana's that'll put him at the scene. 'Course we have to catch him in order to print him."

Based on his conversation with Motherwell, Collins was having misgivings. "Have you completely ruled out all of Lam's artist friends?"

"What are you driving at, Pat?"

"The outfit. It has nothing to do with Santería." He related what Motherwell had told him and showed him the drawing.

"Damn, that adds another wrinkle, all right," admitted O'Connell. "An exquisite corpse, you say? Christ, what a bunch of loonies to dream up something like that. But who would want to turn Lam into a 3-D version of one of those weird doodles?"

"That's what I'm getting at," said Collins. "Other than a Surrealist, who would even know what an exquisite corpse is?"

FIFTY-FIVE.

No sooner had the Port of New York Authority office opened at 8:30 a.m. than Hare's call had been answered. He had concocted a story about expecting some important papers that someone was hand carrying from Cartagena but hadn't been delivered. The ship was supposed to arrive on Friday.

"That'd be the *Princesa*." the clerk informed him. "She was delayed by bad weather. Didn't make port until Saturday."

"Do you know what time she docked?"

"Let's see. just a minute, I need to check the clearance log." He put down the phone. and Hare fidgeted while the clerk consulted the listings. "Here it is." he reported. "Clearance was at 8:45 p.m. Saturday. Your papers could have come off any time after that."

Hare thanked him and hung up. Damn it, clearance is right—that clears Solana. According to Breton. Lam was dead before the sailor even stepped ashore.

Abruptly disconnected, the clerk realized that the caller hadn't given his name or mentioned anything about the nature of the documents he was expecting. Early in the afternoon, he received a bulletin about the same ship, which had left port that morning. Confirm current position and route while in U.S. waters, it said. Gosh, he thought,

165

they must be planning to intercept her. I guess those papers weren't delivered after all. They must be pretty important.

He imagined something so sensitive that it couldn't be trusted to radio or telegraphic transmission, maybe intelligence about refueling points for the U-boats that were making such a hash of trade routes to and from southern waters.

Once again he cursed the myopia that had kept him out of the military and dreamed of the heroic deeds he would have done if allowed to serve. Once again he consoled himself with the knowledge that he was doing his bit on the home front, helping to keep what commercial shipping there was running as efficiently as conditions permitted. Not everyone in the office was as conscientious as he.

He set aside the manifest he was checking and looked up the *Princesa*'s return route to South America. She had loaded up with agricultural machinery and parts, and had no scheduled stops between New York and Cartagena, so she would have to be intercepted at sea. This is an important assignment, he decided, and I'll see to it that the ship doesn't leave our territorial waters with those papers.

To save fuel during wartime, cargo ships were steaming at reduced speeds. A trip that normally took six days direct now took eight or nine, as freighters hugged the coast to steer as clear of U-boats as possible. Judging by the clock, the clerk calculated that the *Princesa*'s rough position was no more than sixty miles out of port, well north of Atlantic City and still inside the three-mile limit. Plenty of time to get a Coast Guard cutter from the Atlantic City station to intercept.

He pictured himself on the cutter's bridge, trumpeting orders to the boarding party. He got on the horn to the radio room, determined to retrieve the documents that he now believed were vital to the war effort.

"Hello. Sparky, this is George," he announced. "I've got an urgent message for the *Princesa*. She left port at 7:00 a.m., and will be abreast of Barnegat about now. Alert her to prepare for boarding by the Coast Guard. Get her coordinates and speed and radio that information to the station down at AC, tell them to get ready to scramble."

Suddenly he curbed himself. "I'll get back to you with more details." He realized with alarm that he had no idea just what the Coast Guard should be looking for, who had the papers, whatever they were, or where on board they might be. He had jumped the gun, seriously exceeded his authority, in fact.

"Not necessary. George," Sparky reassured him. "All I needed was her approximate position, so I can tell the FBI which Coast Guard station to notify. I'm to radio the ship, and the Feds'll take it from there."

Both thrilled and relieved, the clerk felt his heart jump. So it really was something of national importance if the FBI was involved. And he was responsible for setting the operation in motion! He would never learn the outcome—of course, they would have to keep the whole thing under wraps—but he would have the satisfaction of knowing that he had played his part.

He sighed with pleasure, cleaned his thick eyeglasses, and went back to checking the manifest.

FIFTY-SIX.

"He didn't do it."

Hare was sitting on the couch in Matta's living room, talking more to the floor than to his host, who was seated on a chair opposite, practically knee-to-knee with him. Hare was keeping his voice down so as not to disturb Anne and the twins in the bedroom. The bedroom door had been open when he arrived, and Anne had glanced up from her diaper-changing task and seen him come in, but Matta quickly closed the door on her.

That move didn't surprise Anne. He had been jumpy ever since his argument with that horrible sailor. Sulking in the studio after the man left. Running out and coming back without a word last night, then hardly touching his breakfast this morning, just coffee and cigarettes until Hare showed up.

Something had gone wrong with the scheme, she knew, but what? She could only pray that it had fallen through. Maybe the drugs never came, maybe Carlos couldn't get them after all. I guess Fredo was telling the truth. That's why Roberto and David are so upset. Please, God, let that be the end of it.

"I talked to Breton last night," Hare continued. "He told me that Lam was dead by around 8:00 p.m., no later. With his medical training, I'm sure he knows what he's talking about. I found out that the crew wasn't cleared to leave the ship until 8:45. Carlos couldn't have gotten to the apartment before 9:00."

Matta sat back, taking in this information. Keeping his voice low, he replied, "Okay, so Carlos really did find him dead, and really did dress him up to throw suspicion away from himself. Naturally he takes the money. Naturally he takes the coke to sell elsewhere. All that makes sense, once you know he didn't kill Lam. But who did?"

Suddenly Hare had another thought.

"How do we know he was killed?"

"What are you talking about? The police said he didn't die of natural causes."

"That was yesterday, when they first questioned us, right after his body was discovered. I bet they didn't have a medical report by then. They just assumed that, because of the costume, someone killed him and dressed him up like that. But there's another explanation." Hare was warming to his theory.

"Breton said there were no visible wounds, in fact no evidence of violence at all. Maybe he actually had a heart attack."

Matta was stunned. "Jesus, do you really think . . ."

"Who had a heart attack?"

Anne's voice seemed to echo in the room. For one guilty moment she hoped it was Carlos they were talking about. That would solve the problem once and for all.

Both men were startled to see her emerge from the bedroom, they hadn't heard the door open. They looked at each other, unsure of what to say or who should say it. Hare lowered his eyes. After all, Matta was her husband, it was his responsibility to decide whether to make up an explanation or tell the truth, or perhaps part of it.

Matta's annoyance at her meddling gave way to some quick thinking. He decided to be as truthful as possible without actually saying anything.

"We're not sure that's what it was, dear. David and I have some checking to do. I'll let you know as soon as we have news."

They rose quickly and made their escape, leaving Anne still in the dark.

Monday evening

FIFTY-SEVEN.

Commissioner Valentine had other, more urgent matters to occupy him that day, so it wasn't until early evening, as he was about to leave the office, that he remembered to ring Peggy Guggenheim with the good news. He was lucky to catch her at home, preparing for a rendezvous at Café Society Uptown on East 58th Street, where she was hoping to find her husband without a female companion. With Max, you never knew who might attach herself to his adhesive embrace. Their marriage had been fractious from the start, but she had a fine appreciation of his charismatic charm, as well as enormous respect for him as an artist and sympathy for his situation as a de facto enemy alien.

To Americans in wartime, every German was automatically suspect, no matter that the Nazis had interned Max when Hitler's forces overran France. His art was labeled degenerate, and even though he wasn't Jewish he might as well have been, since he was lumped with the Jews, gypsies, and other undesirables marked for extermination. He probably would have been sent to a death camp if he hadn't escaped and she hadn't helped spirit him out of Europe.

171

After Pearl Harbor, Max had to register with the government, and Peggy decided that marriage to an American would help shield him from harassment. She was wrong. After a disastrous vacation trip to Cape Cod, where the FBI questioned Max, practically accused him of being a Nazi spy, and warned him to stay away from the coast, they retreated to the relative safety of New York City, where the sympathetic art world offered some measure of protection. Lam's death had opened that world to scrutiny by the authorities. All the Surrealist émigrés, Max included, were under suspicion. So were any Americans who associated with them.

But now, as Peggy dressed for the evening, she reflected happily on Valentine's report. The Surrealists were in the clear. She decided to wear her favorite Fortuny gown—an extravagant acquisition from her early days in Paris that still fit her twenty years later—and declare a celebration. The nightclub's owner, Barney Josephson, might even be persuaded to donate a bottle of prewar champagne. A first-generation American, son of Latvian immigrants, he welcomed the European exiles, whose lively banter in French added tone to the sophisticated atmosphere he cultivated.

Josephson greeted her warmly as she swept in. A Continental-style kiss on each cheek, an admiring appraisal of her outfit, and a gentlemanly offer to take her wrap. "You look like a million bucks," he told her, "but then, so does your uncle Solomon."

"You know I'm just a poor relation, Barney," she replied amiably, "not to mention the family's black sheep. That's why I come to your club, you let us blacks in."

In addition to its reputation as one of the city's hottest jazz spots, Café Society Uptown was known for its integrated clientele. Josephson was proud of the fact that Negroes and whites mixed backstage, onstage, and out front. The club's program also broke the mold. On

Mondays, when many nightclubs were dark, he featured some of the most prominent entertainers. Tonight Art Tatum was at the piano, warming up the crowd for Lena Horne, the beautiful vocalist who got her start at Josephson's downtown club—another reason Peggy might expect to see Max in the audience.

Sure enough, she spotted him at a table with her ex-husband Laurence Vail, his ex-wife Kay Boyle, and Kay's new husband, Baron Joseph von Franckenstein, an anti-Nazi Austrian aristocrat serving in the OSS.

Seated next to Max was his son Hans, known as Jimmy, who was acting as Peggy's assistant at Art of This Century. Jimmy was a big fan of American jazz and relished the opportunity to hang out with his famous father, who was more interested in the singer, in town with Duke Ellington's orchestra to promote her new film, "Stormy Weather," than in her music.

"Will you do me a favor, Barney?" Peggy asked. "We have something to celebrate tonight, and I'd like a bottle of champagne for the table. If you'll bring one over, please join us."

Josephson took the hint. Peggy was a good customer—a generous one when she'd had a few drinks—so one bottle on the house would probably lubricate the wheels.

"It will be my pleasure, Peggy darling," he cooed. "Let me show you to your table and I'll be along directly."

173

FIFTY-EIGHT.

"What are we celebrating?" asked Kay. "Joseph and I have been married for a month, but if you want to toast our future happiness we'll drink to that!"

"Bonne santé, mes chères, et nombreux retours heureux." replied Peggy as she raised her glass. "But as delighted as I am for you both, your marriage isn't the occasion." She was savoring the suspense and planned to draw it out as long as possible.

It was a remarkable gathering that hung on her words. In spite of their complicated relationships, they remained bonded, with Peggy as the glue.

Vail, the son of American expatriates, had been her first husband, a dashing man about town who had swept her off her feet when she arrived in Paris as a headstrong twenty-three-year-old heiress seeking adventure. He deflowered her, wedded her, and fathered her two children. Sinbad and Pegeen. Although they had been divorced for many years, he was financially dependent on her.

A talented writer and artist, Vail was a heavy drinker whose indolent nature interfered with any sort of serious career, much less gainful employment. He was also far from monogamous. His affair with Boyle, an American writer, had begun while he and Peggy were married, but since she was equally promiscuous, she accepted the

174

situation as a consequence of the bohemian expatriate life she had embraced. So Peggy supported them both.

But after Kay and Laurence married, she had turned the tables by falling in love with von Franckenstein during the early days of the war, when his outspoken opposition to the Hitler regime had made him a marked man in Austria. Taking refuge in Paris, he was looking for a way to aid the Allied cause when he and Kay met and became lovers. In those turbulent times, when the present was perilous and the future bleak, they were soon parted, but found each other again in New York.

The baron had offered his services to the American army, which had brought him to the States for training. After many setbacks and delays, in July 1941 Peggy had managed to secure passage on the Pan American Clipper for Laurence, Kay, Max, and seven of their respective children—except for Jimmy, who had arrived in New York two years earlier. Now they all were reunited, savoring their escape from the Nazis and eager to celebrate whatever Peggy was proposing.

Max was becoming restive. "Au nom de dieu, explique!" he demanded. The others seconded him. Once Lena Horne began to sing, their conversation would be interrupted.

"All right, I won't keep you guessing," she began. "First, I must tell you that this is a bittersweet occasion, equal parts sadness and happiness. I only wish Marcel were here to share it, for he was the messenger of the bad news."

Now they were anxious, also somewhat fearful that the bad news involved a setback for the Allies or perhaps word that Sinbad, who had been drafted, was about to ship out.

"I don't mean to alarm you, but Wifredo Lam died on Saturday. The tragic loss of a dear friend and a great artist."

Murmurs from around the table expressed shock and sincere regrets.

Peggy explained the circumstances as related to her by Duchamp, including the exquisite corpse costume. To describe the reaction as stunned would be an understatement.

"If the police had understood its meaning," she continued, "they would have concluded that Fredo was killed by a Surrealist. Why, they might have arrested Max! Fortunately they had no idea what it meant, and in any case it proved to be a diversion, as Marcel and I assumed. As soon as he told me, I telephoned the police commissioner, a friend of the family, and asked him to take a personal interest in the case. He rang me half an hour ago with the good news." She paused for effect.

"The killer has been identified. Not a Surrealist. That is what we are celebrating." She raised her glass and drank, enjoying the party's rapt attention.

"Well," said Laurence, "are we going to learn his identity? It is a he, I assume."

"Yes, it's a man, a sailor Fredo befriended on the boat from Cuba. They would get together when he was in port. It turns out that he is a smuggler. The police think Fredo found out his friend was a criminal and they had an argument. The sailor hit him on the head, not meaning to kill him, but the blow was fatal. He used the costume to throw the police off his trail."

"What do you mean, they think that's what happened?" asked the baron. "Haven't they arrested him, questioned him?"

"Unfortunately, no." Peggy explained. "He shipped out this morning, before they identified him. It's a Colombian vessel bound for Cartagena. They are going to radio the ship and asked to have him put ashore somewhere en route. If the captain cooperates, they can arrest him and bring him back to New York."

"That's a big if," said Josephson, "but at least you know who the killer is and your people are in the clear. That's certainly worth celebrating. I'll have another bottle of the '38 Moët sent over." As the house lights dimmed, he excused himself and stepped onto the bandstand.

"She first thrilled you at Café Society Downtown," he began, "and now, on the silver screen, she's captivating audiences around the country. But she prefers a warm welcome at our humble club to all the Hollywood razzle-dazzle. Ladies and gentlemen, Miss Lena Horne."

Amid enthusiastic applause, as a golden spotlight escorted the singer to the microphone, Jimmy leaned over, tucked two fingers under Max's chin, and gently closed his gaping mouth.

FIFTY-NINE.

Yun Gee walked up Seventh Avenue and turned east on 8th Street. The Cedar Tavern beckoned. Just a couple of drinks, he decided, just a round or two with the boys. He was getting too old to punish himself as he had been doing, and Helen probably wouldn't put up with it much longer. Plus he was nearly broke. His part-time war work as a mechanical drafter at Bell Labs on West Street kept him and the family going, but payday wasn't until Friday.

He spotted Motherwell, who lived only a few doors away, at the round table in the rear. With him were Pollock, apparently deep in thought, and de Kooning, who motioned Gee to join them. He grabbed a beer at the bar and pulled up a chair.

Brief greetings were followed by a return to the topic of the week. Motherwell had been feeling guilty about his revelation to Collins, which he feared would spark a new round of probing in the art community. But no one else had heard anything more from the police, as far as they knew.

"How about you, Yun?" asked Pollock. "You were pretty tight with Lam. The cops been onto you?"

Gee told them about his Chinatown inquiry.

"If Lam double-crossed one of the tongs, they would certainly kill him. Their errand boy told me they didn't, but I don't know if that's true. They settle their own scores."

His listeners nodded as if they understood the arcane workings of the Chinese underworld.

"Why would they dress him as an exquisite corpse?" asked Motherwell, "and how would they know what that signifies?"

Gee was confused. He wasn't familiar with the term and O'Connell hadn't described the costume to him. Motherwell, who had just been telling his friends about Collins's follow-up visit, explained.

"Lam was turned into a parody of a Surrealist parlor game? I need another drink," said Gee, "a real one." He went to the bar and ordered a whiskey. He had just enough money for a double.

SIXTY.

O'Connell entered Collins's office without knocking, startling the detective as he pondered the crime scene photographs one more time.

"They've got him!" thundered O'Connell, planting himself opposite Collins and treating him to a self-satisfied smile. "Solana. The Coast Guard took him off the ship this afternoon. Didn't need the FBI after all."

"Why not? Wasn't he outside our jurisdiction?"

"Yes, for the homicide charge, but smuggling interdiction is a Coast Guard responsibility, so that's what they charged him with."

"Does that mean we won't get to question him?"

"They'll get first crack," O'Connell explained, "but they won't be able to make the charge stick. He's on his way out empty, and you can bet that whatever he got paid, he hasn't got it on him. It's probably penny-ante stuff anyway. They wouldn't even have bothered with him if he weren't a homicide suspect. No, they'll have to turn him loose, but they'll do it in the Port of New York. They're bringing him back here tonight. Probably dock at the Staten Island station, or maybe Sheepshead Bay."

"He can cool his heels in the Coast Guard brig overnight," reflected Collins. "I'll find out where they're holding him in the morning."

"Better phone the 23rd and get one of the Spanish-speaking officers to go with you to pick him up," O'Connell advised. "Detective Morales, if he's available. I watched him question that gunrunner we collared in Harlem last year. He played that bastard like a violin, and he called the tune."

"You think we can make him for manslaughter?" asked Collins. "I don't see murder, myself. After all, he didn't even rob the guy, so he didn't kill him for the money. My guess is he made a stupid mistake and tried to throw us off with that Surrealist diversion. I hope Morales can get a coherent story out of him."

He picked up the telephone and asked to be put through to the 23rd Precinct. Morales was off duty, but the desk sergeant told Collins that Officer Diaz was available. She came on the line and Collins filled her in.

"This is excellent news, Detective Collins," she said. He could hear the satisfaction in her voice. "Detective Morales will be back on duty in the morning, and I'm sure he'll be delighted to accompany you. He's the one who traced Solana's connection to Lam."

"Great," Collins replied. "Ask him to call me when he gets in. Meanwhile I'll get the location where they're holding Solana and we can meet there."

He was about to ring off when Nita asked, "Mind if I tag along?" Before he could object, she continued, "If Hector—Detective Morales, I mean—says I can? I'm thinking of putting in for detective, and he's kind of a mentor to me. He's always telling me to learn from experience, not from the textbooks. I promise not to say anything. I'll just be a fly on the wall."

Collins agreed reluctantly. "Well, if it's okay with Morales, it's okay with me."

SIXTY-ONE.

Hare and Matta had spent the day trying to find out more about the investigation. They were having no luck. They crisscrossed Greenwich Village, tramping from one walkup to another, learning nothing more than they already knew. Everyone who had been questioned by the police was told the same meager story, no details, nothing about the exquisite corpse disguise.

The only one they couldn't find was Motherwell. He was out when they called, and Maria didn't know where he was or when he'd be back. When they finally reached him by telephone that evening, he mentioned that Collins had been to see him again.

"When did he come back, and why?" Hare wanted to know.

"He was here this morning," said Motherwell. "He had a question about the crime scene that he thought I could answer. I'm afraid I did answer it, and in doing so opened a can of worms."

"What do you mean?"

"Lam's body was decorated. Whoever killed him used things in the studio to make him look like an exquisite corpse. Before I realized that it would implicate a Surrealist, I told Collins what it was." Motherwell was surprised to learn that Hare wasn't shocked.

"I know about the costume. Duchamp told me." It had been Matta, but he couldn't give that away. "Did Collins say anything about the cause of death?"

"Yes. He had the autopsy results. Lam was struck on the head."

Hare groaned inwardly. So much for his heart attack theory.

"Are you there, David?"

"Yes, yes, I'm here. Just wondering what this means for us." Especially for me, he mused, and even more especially for Matta, who was sitting beside him anxiously waiting to learn what Motherwell had said.

"Thanks, Bob. I'll be in touch." He rang off.

"It looks bad," he told Matta, "unless we can implicate Carlos." The only way out was to pin the blame on him. They started to work out a plan.

Hare said that Matta, who was closest to Lam, should to go to the police and finger Solana. Tell them that the sailor was Lam's pal, that he was in port on the evening of the killing, and that he knew what an exquisite corpse was because he sometimes hung out with Lam's artist friends. Then again, better not mention that he's a sailor, that'll make it harder to find him.

Matta began to rehearse the story. "I'll say Lam had a friend, a Cuban guy named Carlos. I don't know his last name. I never met him. He's from out of town. He would visit Lam whenever he came to New York. Lam found out he was involved in some kind of criminal activity, and he was very upset about it. He told me he was expecting Carlos this weekend and was going to confront him. They must have gotten into a fight about it, and Carlos hit him too hard. I can say I heard from Motherwell that he was killed by a blow to the head. Then Carlos tried to cover his tracks with the Surrealist costume."

That part was true.

"Carlos will be presumed guilty, and by the time they figure out who he is, he'll be long gone. I can get word to him via the Cartagena contact that he's wanted for murder. He wouldn't be foolish enough to come back to New York with that hanging over him. That way we'll be in the clear." Hare nodded his agreement.

The only flaw they could find in this scenario was the timing. Once the police identified Solana, how closely would they check the time of death against his arrival on the *Princesa*?

Maybe there was enough leeway. They'd have to take that chance.

Tuesday morning, October 19

SIXTY-TWO.

Over good coffee and excellent croissants, which he had picked up on the way to Peggy's, Duchamp heard all about the previous evening's party at Café Society Uptown.

"Isn't it wonderful, Luigi, they've solved the case already!" Peggy gushed. "I'm so glad I had the presence of mind to call the commissioner. I'm sure it made all the difference."

Duchamp sipped his café au lait. "You are remarkable, cherie. Friends in high places and lovers in low ones," he teased.

Her rejoinder was on target. "And how shall I classify you, who fit both categories?"

He chuckled and replied, "touché."

She stroked his arm affectionately. "Is that an invitation?"

"Pas pendant le petit dejeuner, je t'en prie. Romance interferes with my digestion."

Peggy interrupted their erotic banter with another announcement. "I've heard back from the United States Embassy in Havana," she told him. "A telegram arrived just before you did. They located Helena at the home of Lam's relatives. The family was told that Wifredo was found dead in his studio, but nothing was said about the circumstances. What could they say, except that they would be kept informed of developments?"

Peggy sighed. "How horrible it must be for her, so far away, alone with his grieving family. I must help her. Tell me, Luigi, you know them better than I—were they close, Fredo and Helena? Did they love each other, did he respect her, encourage her?"

Duchamp had always resisted pitying Peggy, since many of her woes were self-inflicted and she had enough money to make even her misery comfortable. But now, seeing the reflection of her relationship with Max in her curiosity about Helena's situation, he felt sympathy for her. If only she could have found in Max the kind of soul mate Helena had in Lam.

"It was a love match, I am certain," he said. "Any comfort you can give her will be a blessing."

Impulsive as ever, Peggy jumped up from the table, charged across the room to the telephone, and dialed Harry Guggenheim, a son of Peggy's uncle Daniel. Harry had been the United States Ambassador to Cuba in the early 1930s.

"Hello, Harry dear? Peggy here. Are you well? Oh, good. Yes, I'm fine, thank you. It's been too long since you and Alicia came to dine, and I hope we can do it one day soon, but I'm actually calling to ask a favor."

Unfortunately, cousin Harry couldn't guarantee to secure immediate passage for Helena. Apart from the difficulty of arranging travel during wartime, she was a German national and she and Lam were not legally married.

"Why are these things always so complicated?" complained Peggy. "No one who took one look at Helena Holzer could possibly imagine her as a dangerous enemy. She's as meek as a mouse and completely non-political. Can't you pull some strings?"

"My dear Peggy, I'm not a magician, and I've been out of the diplomatic corps for ten years," Harry reminder her gently. The last thing he wanted was an argument with his imperious cousin, who evidently believed that the Guggenheim name was enough to unlock doors that were closed to ordinary mortals. "I know you haven't forgotten that we're at war."

"Not with Cuba, as far as I'm aware."

"No, of course not. Cuba's our most valuable Caribbean ally against the Axis. But we *are* at war with Germany, and so is Cuba. I'm sure this Holzer woman is under surveillance. Look at the trouble Max has had, and he's married to an American citizen, and a Guggenheim to boot. What chance is there that our government will admit an enemy alien, the common-law widow of a refugee, even one vouched for by a Guggenheim?"

"They let Max in," she persisted, "and we weren't married then."

Harry gave in. "Oh, all right, I'll see what I can do. Or rather what can be done under the circumstances. I'll put my secretary on, and you can give him the woman's address and whatever other information you think may strengthen the case. I'll personally pass the request along to Ambassador Braden. We can try for admission on compassionate grounds."

Peggy offered to pay Helena's passage as she had done for the other European refugees she sponsored.

"Don't worry about that," said Harry. "I can get an aeroplane. It's only a short hop, 229 air miles, from Havana to Miami. From there it's 1,089 air miles to Floyd Bennett Field. The whole trip can be done in a day if the weather's good, two at the most. I did it often when I was posted to Cuba."

With a lifelong passion for aeronautics, Guggenheim—who had served with distinction as a navy pilot during the Great War—had connections to aviators, both civilian and military, around the country. One phone call, and a plane and pilot would be at his disposal.

"Getting her out is no problem," he assured her. "The problem will be getting her in."

SIXTY-THREE.

"Who had a heart attack?

Anne repeated the question she had first asked yesterday morning. She was clearing the breakfast dishes, while Matta sat at the kitchen table smoking and finishing his coffee. She had left the bedroom door open so she could monitor the twins, who had been fed and changed and were gurgling happily in their double crib.

He realized he'd have to tell her something, she obviously wasn't going to drop it, and she was bound to find out sooner or later that Lam was dead. He decided to try a version of the story that he and Hare had rehearsed. He also decided to turn on the charm that lately had been in such short supply.

"Pajarito, dearest, come and sit by me, please." He had not called her little bird, his affectionate nickname for her, in quite some time. His voice spoke of concern, for her and for the subject he was about to broach.

"I'll tell you, but first I want to apologize for the way I've been acting. You see, I've been preoccupied, very worried about Fredo. He's gotten involved in a bad business, something illegal. I don't know the details, but that sailor who was here was his partner."

You're not telling me anything I don't already know, and you're lying about not knowing the details, said

189

Anne to herself. You were in it with Fredo, and so was David. She could feel her emotions rising, but tried to keep her expression neutral and attentive while she heard him out.

He reached over and took her hands in his.

"The sailor, Carlos, told me that he went to Fredo's apartment and found him dead."

Anne flinched. "Dead," she whispered. Her eyes stopped focusing on her husband's winsome face and went blank.

Matta patted her hands and continued. "He said he had no idea what happened to Fredo. He doesn't speak English, and he knew we were friends, so he came to me for advice. Frankly, I thought he might have killed him—that's why I got so upset and angry. He denied it, of course. I told him to go to the devil. Then later I got to thinking that maybe Carlos was telling the truth, maybe it was a heart attack. That's what David and I were talking about when you came in."

Anne had gone completely still. He thought she had stopped breathing, and in fact for a few moments she had. The color had drained from her face, and when she did take a breath it was short and shallow.

She was in shock.

"My God, Pajarito, your hands are like ice."

Matta rose, lifted her out of her chair, and led her toward the bedroom.

"Now you see why I was reluctant to tell you. I knew you'd be upset." Not this upset, he thought. His concern was genuine. Could she have a weak heart? They'd been married for four years, surely he would have known.

He sat her down on the bed and removed her shoes. "Lie down and rest, darling," he suggested. She didn't move, so he gently eased her up to standing, pulled back the covers, sat her down again, and put her under.

"I have to go out for a little while, not long. You stay there, keep an eye on the boys for me, will you?" he asked, hoping her motherly instinct would help her snap out of her trance. Her eyes flickered, but she didn't answer.

He left quietly, mentally reviewing the story he was about to tell the police, anxious to get it behind him.

Tuesday midday

SIXTY-FOUR.

Fitz did a double take as the party entered the 6th Precinct lobby. Detective Collins led the way, followed by a disheveled and dejected-looking character, apparently a sailor. wearing a pea jacket. a watch cap. and handcuffs. Behind him came a large Hispanic man in plain clothes, accompanied by a uniformed officer. none other than Nita. Her luxuriant red hair was tucked discreetly under her visor cap. and she had assumed the alert. watchful attitude befitting a police escort.

Fitz approached the group as they neared the desk. Nita saw him coming. smiled faintly, and cocked her head. They both stepped off a few paces while Collins handled the booking procedure.

"Officer Diaz. what a surprise. It's good to see you again," he began, forcefully suppressing the urge to greet her with a kiss.

"A pleasure. Officer Fitzgerald," she replied with equal formality while her eyes spoke more eloquently than her voice. "I'm here with Detective Hector Morales. my colleague from the 23rd, to question a suspect in the Lam case. He speaks no English. so Collins asked for Hector to translate. I think O'Connell told him what a great interrogator Hector is. I asked if I could observe, and they said okay, so here I am, bringing up the rear."

The formalities at the desk concluded, Collins marched Carlos Solana down the hall to an interrogation room. Fitz followed, reluctant to abandon his position beside Nita.

"Fitzgerald," Collins ordered, "get Jeff to bring in the fingerprint kit and the stenotype."

"Yes, sir," said Fitz, as he opened the door for them.

"Didn't the Coast Guard print him?" asked Morales. Even in a normal tone of voice, his resonant baritone rang with authority.

"I suppose they did," Collins replied, "but they didn't offer to turn them over to us. At least they let us copy his particulars off his merchant seaman's registration papers. Officially he's charged with smuggling, so I guess we should be grateful that we got the man himself. We can get another set of prints, but there's only one of him."

They filed into the room, and Nita stationed herself unobtrusively in a dimly lighted corner. The only light in the room came from a central overhead lamp above a bare rectangular table. The table was pulled slightly off center, so that the suspect's chair was under the light, but not the interrogator's. This shift put the suspect at a deliberate disadvantage—not unlike the tactic the shadowy On Leong boss had used on Yun Gee.

They waited while the clerk took Solana's fingerprints and set up his stenotype at one end of the table. Solana was escorted to the hot seat in the center, and Morales seated himself opposite, while Collins pulled up a chair next to the clerk and settled down. He dictated the preamble, noting that Detective Morales would conduct the interview in Spanish and would translate the questions and answers into English.

Solana had spoken not a word since they collected him from the Coast Guard station on Staten Island. He had ridden the ferry to Manhattan in silence, staring wistfully at the North River piers lined with vessels that could have taken him far beyond the law's reach. Ever since they pulled him off the *Princesa*, only six hours after she left Pier 52, he had been trying to figure out how they had identified him so quickly. Surely no one in Joey's organization had informed on him—they had a lucrative business deal. But it was the smuggling that got him caught. How could the authorities know?

The only way was Matta, he decided. Matta must have turned me in. He knew all about the cocaine deal—shit, he arranged it! He didn't believe me when I told him I didn't kill Lam. So he fingered me for that, too.

The fear, anger, and self-pity that had kept Solana silent all morning were masked by his blank expression. He had decided that his only option was to say as little as possible, to deny whatever they accused him of—as he had done at the Coast Guard station—and hope that whoever actually did kill Lam would turn up. He kept his downcast eyes focused on the tabletop as Morales studied him dispassionately.

When the detective spoke, it was not in the harsh, intimidating voice Solana had expected. His tone was somehow reassuring, and the sailor glanced up for a moment before retreating into impassivity. Unlike some members of the force, Morales preferred to probe gently rather than badger, though he was not averse to scare tactics and misdirection when circumstances warranted.

Collins couldn't understand the language, but he knew he was watching a master at work.

SIXTY-FIVE.

Loitering in the lobby, making small talk with the desk sergeant, Fitz had been sidelined from the case. He had no cause to be resentful, he knew that, but nevertheless he wished he could be in on the questioning of the prime suspect. He was scheduled to go out on patrol at 2:00 p.m., so he probably wouldn't be around when Nita came out, which bothered him even more than missing the interrogation. He was about to head for the squad room when a man entered, approached the desk, and asked to see Detective Collins. He spoke with a Spanish accent.

"He's not available right now." Ryan told him. "Can Officer Fitzgerald here help you?"

"I'd rather wait for Collins," the man replied. "How long will it be, do you think?"

"Could be quite a while." said Fitz. "What's the nature of your business?"

"I have some information for him. A case he's working on."

"Which case is that?"

"I'll wait to speak to Collins."

Fitz decided to persist. "If you'll tell me which case, I'll get word to him. Find out when he can see you."

"The Lam killing."

He was not surprised to hear the man refer to Lam's killing instead of his death. Word must be all over the Village by now. "What's your name?" he inquired.

"Roberto Matta. Collins came to see me on Sunday. I'm a friend of Lam's. Was, that is."

Fitz took this information down the hall to the interview room. He cracked the door and caught Collins's eye, avoiding Nita's quizzical look. Quietly, Collins slipped outside and listened to what Fitz had to say.

"Interesting," he muttered. "I thought that bird knew more than he was letting on. Maybe I'd better see him now. I'm not doing any good in there." He followed Fitz back to the lobby, where Matta waited on a hard bench opposite the desk. The artist rose and extended his hand.

"Thanks for coming in, Mr. Matta," said Collins as they shook. "Let's step into my office." They left Fitz, excluded once again, in the lobby.

Ten minutes later, the desk sergeant's intercom buzzed. "It's Collins. He wants you," he told Fitz.

Fitz knocked on the office door and entered. Collins beckoned him to his desk and handed him several sheets of paper covered with his scrawled handwriting.

"Have Mr. Matta's statement typed up, Officer Fitzgerald. If the clerk is occupied," which Collins knew he was, "find someone who can take care of it. I want it for him to sign as soon as possible."

"Yes, sir, I'll see to it right away," Fitz replied. He hurried down the hall and into the clerk's office, where he busied himself at the typewriter. No way was he going to pass this along to anyone else, even if the best he could do was hunt and peck. He had actually learned typing in high school, and even though he was rusty he managed more quickly than he had expected, especially given Collins's bad penmanship. Once that was deciphered, the complete statement filled only a single typed page.

196

It began with the artist's full name. He had spelled it out for Collins at the top of the first page of handwritten notes: Roberto Sebastián Antonio Matta Echaurren. Fitz snickered. "Bet his mama don't call him that, except when she's really mad at him," he said under his breath. "Like I hear Brian Francis Xavier Fitzgerald from my ma when she's sending me to the doghouse."

He let out more snickers as he read and transcribed the notes. "So you don't know what Carlos' last name is? Well, we do. Or what he does for a living? We know that, too. Or where to find him? He's right here in this station house, not thirty feet from where you're sitting."

Matta had repeated the story he and Hare concocted after Hare's conversation with Motherwell. They had refined it until it got so plausible that they almost believed it themselves. The fact that it was based on truths and half-truths made it that much easier to tell convincingly. The only real pitfall was the role they had played in the smuggling scheme, but he wasn't about to let that slip. And Carlos wasn't around to contradict him. Or so he believed.

In less than fifteen minutes, Fitz was back in the detective's office with the statement ready for Matta's signature. Collins took the paper from Fitz, glanced at it and handed it to Matta. "Please read this over, Mr. Matta, and sign it if you approve. If you make any changes, please initial them."

The artist spent a few moments reviewing the typescript. He crossed out a word, initialed it, signed the paper, and handed it to Collins.

"I corrected myself, I hope you don't mind. I said that Lam was very furious at Carlos, but I think just furious is better."

"That's fine, Mr. Matta. Just furious it is." Collins rose from his chair, Matta did likewise, and they shook hands again.

"Thank you for coming in," said Collins amiably. "You've been very helpful, and we'll get working on this information right away." He gestured to Fitz, who kept his mouth shut as he escorted their snitch out to the lobby. It was nearly 2:00 p.m., time for him to hit the beat. He decided to give Matta a head start then follow him. Just out of curiosity.

7uesday afternoon

SIXTY-SIX.

After the prisoner was led away, Morales and Collins conferred while the clerk packed up his stenotype machine and Nita continued to observe.

"I gotta hand it to you, Morales," said Collins admiringly, "I thought he was going to clam up completely, but you managed to get more out of him than I think he realized."

"Mostly just a broken record, no señor, no señor, no señor," said Morales, "but having Matta's statement certainly was helpful, it really gave me an advantage. Mind you, there are holes in it, big ones. The part about him not knowing anything about Carlos is obviously a crock. As soon as I mentioned his name, I got a rise out of Carlos. He knows Matta well enough to be afraid of him."

"How much of what Matta told me do you believe?" Collins asked.

Morales speculated. "That Lam had a fight with Carlos, no. When I asked Carlos about that, he denied it, and I believe him. Nothing solid to go on, it's just a hunch. That Carlos put the costume on the body, yes. He denied that, too, but I think he was lying. That Carlos is a criminal, yes, but a very small-time crook. All the merchant seamen do a little smuggling on the side, who cares? Certainly not his buddy Lam. No, there had to be more to it than that.

"Carlos needs time to think things over," Morales continued. "If he admits to smuggling, without concrete evidence the worst they can do to him is pull his ticket and deport him, but if he's convicted of manslaughter he'll get prison time. If he claims self-defense, it won't hold up. He's not stupid. I think he'll figure it out and decide to tell the whole story."

Morales stood up and stretched. "You can hold him on a forty-eight-hour warrant. A couple of days in the cooler should loosen his tongue. Meanwhile I have to try to get him a lawyer, he's going to need one. Let's go, Officer Diaz."

Nita, who had been silent since she parted from Fitz in the hall, waited until they were on their way to the subway before asking the question that was stuck in her craw.

"How do you know he was telling the truth about not fighting with Lam? All he said was 'no, señor.' He said the same thing when you asked about the costume, but you didn't believe him that time. Why not?"

"Partly because of the way he said it each time," Morales explained. "After you've questioned as many people as I have, you can hear the little nuances that give them away. You develop a kind of personal built-in lie detector. When he denied fighting, it came out straight, not real emphatic like he was trying to convince me, more matter-of-fact. He kept his eyes down but steady.

"When he denied creating the costume, he was just a bit too insistent. And his eyes shifted just a little. You probably couldn't see it from where you were standing. Maybe you saw his head move, very subtle it was."

"I didn't notice that," Nita admitted. "I was trying to take everything in, but I missed it."

"Most of the time he was as still as a statue, literally scared stiff but in control of himself," said Morales. "I admire his stoicism. But I think he'll soften up."

They walked in silence for a few minutes. Then Nita was pleasantly surprised when Morales asked for her opinion.

"There was something in Matta's statement I didn't understand," he told her. "When I first read it, I thought he called Lam's body an exquisite corpse. That shocked me. Then I realized he was talking about the costume, the disguise, whatever you want to call it. But why call it that?"

"I've certainly never heard a dead body described that way," she said. "At funerals, people will often say the corpse looks peaceful, maybe even beautiful, but exquisite? No, sir."

She thought a moment. "I'll ask Fitz—Officer Fitzgerald, I mean." Suddenly she looked sheepish, and Morales gave her an understanding smile.

"Sweet on him, aren't you?"

"Hector, you're too foxy for me."

SIXTY-SEVEN.

It was only a few blocks from the 6th Precinct station house to Matta's Patchin Place apartment, which is where the artist headed after he left. New York was enjoying a mild, dry autumn. The hurricane that delayed the *Princesa* had drifted east, missed the Atlantic coast and petered out over New Brunswick. On the West Village streets, pushcarts displayed their produce in the afternoon sun, shop doors were propped open invitingly, and the sidewalks were busy with foot traffic. Fitz had no trouble keeping Matta in sight without being obvious. The surveillance was uneventful. A stop in the drugstore on Greenwich then straight home.

Inside the pharmacy, Matta used the pay phone to report to Hare on his visit to the police station.

"I'm glad that's over with," he said. "I hope it will keep them busy for a while, and off our trail for good."

Hare's voice was harsh with anger. "Why the hell did Carlos have to kill him? Surely he could have gotten the money without going that far."

"It was an accident. You should have seen him, he swore up and down he didn't do it, but I could tell he was terrified. Our story really did him a favor. While they're trying to trace him, he can get away clean."

202

"Listen," Matta continued, "I can't talk any more. Anne isn't feeling well and I have to get back."

"What's wrong?" Hare asked.

"Well, I don't really know. She sort of collapsed this morning, just like that. She asked me who we were talking about yesterday—you know, the heart attack—and I told her about Lam. Not the whole story, of course, just that he and Carlos had a fight and I thought maybe Carlos killed him. It threw her for a loop. I put her to bed before I left, and she was just staring at the ceiling. I'm going to ask the druggist for something to bring her around."

After he rang off, Matta went to the counter and consulted the pharmacist.

"You did the right thing," he advised. "Keep her warm, elevate her feet, and let her rest. Most likely she'll be fine after she calms down. But if her heartbeat is rapid and her breathing is shallow, call a doctor, she may need oxygen."

Matta thanked him and went on home.

During the hour he'd been gone, Anne had indeed become calmer. Her initial shock had given way briefly to panic and then subsided into remorse.

Three words were repeating in her head like a drumbeat: *I killed him.*

Saturday midday, October 16

Picking himself up off the studio floor, Lam groped for the chair he sat on to study his work in progress, a wooden ladder-back with a rush seat, and slumped down on it. His vision was blurry, and his head felt as heavy as a rock, except it was hollow and echoed with a pounding rhythm that he recognized as his heartbeat. He thought shaking it might clear it, but decided against that when the slight movement of raising it caused his stomach to lurch.

He stood up slowly, steadying himself on the chair back, and reached for the mantelpiece. He almost missed it, but managed to grab hold of it while he got his balance and his nausea passed. I'd better lie down, he told himself. He still couldn't focus, nor did he remember what had happened to make him so disoriented. The bedroom suddenly seemed very far away, so he sat down again. His mouth was dry, he wanted a drink of water, but the kitchen sink was also out of reach. Maybe just sitting very still was the best thing to do for now.

Presently things began to seem clearer. The pain in his head was settling into a dull throbbing ache, and his vision was returning to normal. But he had no memory of what had transpired from the time he was pacing the room, waiting anxiously for Carlos to arrive, until he came to on the floor. I must have blacked out, he decided. No idea for how long. He was alarmed by the thought that he might have had some kind of seizure. Nothing like that had ever happened to him before. He'd felt dizzy a few times when food was short, but this was a completely different feeling, much more painful and intense.

Then Lam realized that the throbbing was coming from the back of his skull. He reached up, felt the bump, and winced. The skin wasn't broken, but the pain was worst there. Not a stroke after all. Someone must have hit him on the head. *Carlos, who else? But why?* He was still too dazed to figure it out, but if he could get some cold water on his head and into his parched throat, things might improve.

Using the chair as a walker, he worked his way to the kitchen sink and turned on the tap. There was a coffee cup on the drain board, and with a shaking hand he filled it, but thought better of tipping his head to drink. He ran a little water into his cupped hand and managed to get some into his mouth. Gingerly, he moistened a dishtowel and pressed it against the back of his neck. The cool compress was helpful, and soon he felt able to tackle a sip or two of water from the cup. He sat down again, and rested his head in one hand while the other held the wet towel that soothed his pain and allowed him to consider what had happened.

There could be only one explanation. Carlos had arrived, but instead of turning over the package he had slugged Lam and left with the cocaine and the money. I thought he was my friend, the double-crossing bastard, Lam cursed to himself. *What a fool, I thought I could trust him.*

He must have made a better deal with somebody uptown. He's been there, he told me about the bar in Harlem where they have real Cuban beer. Why not just go up there and sell the stuff? Because he could get my money, too. All he had to do was knock me out, take the $300 and leave. Then get as much again, or more, from his uptown pals.

All this reasoning made Lam's head begin to throb again. A new wave of nausea hit him, and he had to stop thinking and rest. He hadn't yet thought to check his back pocket, where the three hundred dollar payment remained unmolested. In fact, his mind was increasingly clouded by the blood that was rapidly flowing into the lining of his brain, where the pressure that would soon kill him was building.

Wednesday morning, October 20

SIXTY-EIGHT.

Raul had lain low for the past two days, waiting for the heat to blow over. Now he was back in Joey Ramirez's office, trying to explain why Detective Morales had let it be known that the cops were no longer interested in him.

Joey was not a happy man. He glared across his desk at the squirming Raul.

"You worthless piece of shit," he hissed, "you spilled your guts to Morales, didn't you?"

Raul mustered enough courage to be indignant, as if he had stood firm against the detective's grilling. "I didn't tell him nothing about the drug deal, boss, I swear. Not a word." The fact that Morales had let him off the hook on that aspect of the case was not mentioned.

"So what did you tell him? Spill it, all of it."

"I told him that Carlos and Lam were buddies, that's all. That Carlos came up here to you because he's Cuban and you're Cuban and he thought you could help him out."

"How would he know about me?"

"Maybe from Tio Julio at the Port of Call. It's right across the street from the dock where his ship tied up."

Joey considered this explanation. "Did Morales buy that?"

"Yeah, sure. Why not? Anyway, I said you gave him some money and told him to get lost. Didn't want nothing to do with no murderer."

"They figure he did kill Lam, didn't just find him dead like he said?"

Raul nodded. "They're looking for Lam's killer, that's all we talked about. Don't care about nothing else."

"So you think Carlos was lying?"

"Yeah, I figure he iced him and robbed him, then came up here to sell you the dope, get paid twice. But I didn't say nothing like that to Morales."

Joey leaned across the desk and fixed his gaze on Raul.

"I'm glad to hear it." His eyes narrowed. "Real glad. From now on, you got an opinion, keep it to yourself unless I ask for it. And if I hear you been blabbing on the street or anywhere else, you're gonna wish you'd never been born. Now get out, and keep your cock-sucking mouth shut!"

"Absolutely, boss, you got it!" blurted Raul with relief. He had prepared himself for much worse abuse.

He was not a prayerful young man, but he now prayed that Carlos had escaped. If they got him, he could lead them straight to Joey and a kilo of cocaine.

SIXTY-NINE.

After a fitful night on a jailhouse cot that was not much worse than his bunk, in a cell shared with a couple of drunks who snored louder than his shipmates, Carlos was running over his options yet again.

Morales had told him that he was entitled to a lawyer and that the Legal Aid Society might provide one at no cost, though he couldn't guarantee that because Solana wasn't a New York City resident. There was some money in the Seamen's Bank that he could draw on, so he wouldn't have to depend on charity. He also had plenty more in his hidey-hole, but of course it was out of reach, well on its way to Colombia by now.

He had no idea how strong the case against him was. They knew he and Lam were friends, and they could match his fingerprints to prove he'd been in Lam's apartment. They knew he was in port when Lam was killed. But why would he do such a thing? He wouldn't, he didn't, but how to prove it?

"You do not have to prove it," his attorney told him. The Legal Aid Society had come through after all, and by mid-afternoon Solana was seated in the interview room, out from under the overhead light, opposite Francisco Ortiz, Esq., who was explaining his rights to him in his native language.

"This is the United States of America, Mr. Solana. You are innocent until proven guilty. The burden of proof is on the police. They can charge you on probable cause, but if they cannot find sufficient evidence they will have to release you."

Carlos was astonished. He stared blankly at Ortiz for several moments, taking in the revelation that they couldn't just lock him up and throw away the key because he was the most likely suspect.

"Do you believe that I did not kill my friend?" he asked.

Ortiz, who had represented more than his share of the mendacious guilty, replied candidly, "It does not matter what I believe, Mr. Solana. All that matters is the evidence. If they find enough to indict you, then whether or not they convict you depends on how well the prosecution makes its case."

"What can we do?"

Ortiz looked over his notes. "First of all, what *you* can do is tell me the whole story. I know you are holding out on me. Whatever you say to me in here is privileged information, do you know what that means?" Solana shook his head. "It means that what you tell your attorney in private cannot be used against you in court. So you had better give me all of it."

"You mean even if I tell you I committed a crime, you do not have to report it?"

"That is correct. You are protected by attorney-client privilege."

Now Carlos was even more amazed. He wondered if this could be true, if he could really trust this stranger who had been sent to him by the police.

"I do not know how things work here," he said. "I do not know you or if what you say is the truth."

Ortiz closed his notebook and rose from his chair. "I understand your position, Mr. Solana, and I do not blame you for being skeptical. Think it over and have someone call me if you decide you want me to represent you."

He handed Solana his business card. walked to the door. and knocked. An officer opened it and showed him out, locking the door behind him.

SEVENTY.

Like Carlos, Anne Matta had spent a restless night, though her bed was soft and comfortable, her husband didn't snore, and her boys were now sleeping through. All afternoon Roberto had been very solicitous, raising her feet as the pharmacist recommended, bringing her a cup of hot tea, and sitting with her until her color returned.

Apart from assuring him that she was feeling much better, she had said very little. All she could think to tell him was, "I really don't know what came over me," a cliché that he found entirely inadequate.

"Has anything like that ever happened to you before?" he asked.

"No, I don't think so," she said vaguely, her voice still not back to normal. She seemed distracted, preoccupied, which he put down to the same concern he was feeling. Worry that there was something seriously wrong with her. How would he cope if she were really ill?

That was not, however, what Anne was worried about.

As the physical shock wore off, she tried to get back on track, at least outwardly. There was the twins' afternoon feeding and changing routine, some shopping to be done, dinner to prepare. She told Roberto that she was fine, it was over. Just a strong reaction to the news about Fredo. So

211

unbelievable, out of the blue like that, it hit her harder than she expected, that's all.

"We still don't know what really happened," he told her. "The police are investigating. I'm sure they'll get to the bottom of it. We just have to be patient."

"Yes, that's right," she said, in the same faraway voice. "Keep an eye on the boys, I won't be gone long. Just need to get a few things from the grocer."

Matta went into the studio and sat looking at his unfinished canvas. He was still in the same spot when Anne returned, and he stayed there while she cooked dinner. They both ate very little and said less. For once he washed up, while she fed, changed, and settled the twins.

They were being remarkably docile, possibly an intuitive response to Anne's mood. Whatever caused it, their detachment mirrored hers, causing a strange atmosphere in the apartment that made Matta even more uneasy. He retreated to the studio, where he stared at his unfinished painting without really seeing it.

It was a travesty of a landscape, the atmosphere clogged with a choking fog that ate away like acid at figures struggling through a morass. It was his response to the war—based not on direct experience, since he had escaped before Europe imploded—but on his deep personal anxiety, his fear that the culture he had embraced, and which had nurtured his nascent creativity, was annihilating itself. The painting actually frightened him, and even as he studied it, he tried to block it from his vision.

He was grateful when bedtime came, and he fell asleep surprisingly quickly. Unlike Anne, who spent the night tormented by the drumbeat that returned as soon as she closed her eyes.

Wednesday afternoon

SEVENTY-ONE.

"Hello, Saidie, it's Peggy here. You really must make up your mind about the Pollock. It's a marvelous little picture, so new, so exciting. I think I told you what Piet Mondrian said about his work, the most interesting thing he's seen in America. I was amazed at Piet's enthusiasm, their aesthetics being such poles apart. Jim Sweeney at the Modern says Pollock's talent is positively volcanic, and he's going to write the essay for the brochure, isn't that fabulous?"

She paused to catch her breath. "His show opens in three weeks, and that painting will be snapped up, I promise you. Why, I might even buy it myself! But you have first choice, dear. You will let me know soon, won't you? And when you are next in New York, we'll have lunch. À bientôt."

Replacing the receiver, Peggy felt confident that she had made a sale. A week earlier, when Mrs. Herbert L. May had come up from Baltimore looking for a Masson, she had gently steered her out of the Surrealist gallery—with its curious curving walls, dramatic lighting, biomorphic furniture, and paintings mounted on rods jutting aggressively toward the viewer—and into the daylight gallery, where she was showcasing work by young

213

American unknowns like Pollock, Motherwell, and Baziotes.

"Saidie," advised Peggy helpfully, "you already have several Massons. Why, you paid the man's passage out of occupied France, he should be giving you paintings for free. Let me show you America's answer to Masson, the next advance beyond Surrealism, in fact. He's going to take the art world by storm."

Beckoning Jimmy to help her, she pulled a canvas from the racks. Not too big, a good starter size for a first-time buyer. Jimmy set the painting on a display stand.

"Pollock calls it *Water Birds*, isn't it stunning?" she asked rhetorically. "I think the water analogy is perfect, don't you? His forms positively swim in a sea of color. So graceful, yet bold, dynamic, full of energy. Knowing your collection, I'm sure it will fit right in."

Peggy signaled for a chair and Jimmy obliged. "Take as much time as you like, Saidie. I have to address some invitations to Pollock's one-man show. It opens on November 9th, and this painting will be in it. Wouldn't it be nice to note in the checklist that it's on loan from you?"

She withdrew discreetly, leaving the young and charming Jimmy to attend the deliberation process. He and May, the daughter of an immigrant from Hesse-Cassel, could converse knowledgeably in German about her renowned collection of abstract and Surrealist art, one that almost rivaled Peggy's. Although Max had left his wife and young son in Cologne in the 1920s to join the Parisian avant-garde, Jimmy had often visited his father and grew up socializing with the artists whose works now populated May's walls. He had plenty of titillating gossip for her eager ears.

Now, a week later, Peggy felt that some gentle pressure was appropriate. If May decided within the next day or two to buy the picture, there was time to include her credit in the printed brochure.

Moments after she had hung up, the telephone rang. My, that was quick, she mused. She raised the receiver expectantly, but it was not Saidie May on the line.

"Peggy, dear, it's Harry. Bad news, I'm afraid. The ambassador won't cooperate."

"Oh, Harry, how disappointing. Have you tried everything?"

"I've spoken directly to Spruille Braden in Havana—it wasn't easy getting a line through, I can tell you—and he's confident that Lam's body can be repatriated to Cuba as soon as the police release it. I told him I would arrange transport and he agreed. But he adamantly opposes allowing Helena Holzer into the United States. He says he can't vouch for her, notwithstanding your assurance that she's harmless, and even if he did recommend her, State Department red tape would hold her up for weeks, with no guarantee of approval. And what good could she do in New York? She's not a suspect, and since they weren't married she has no authority over his remains or his estate. Disposition is up to his family, and Spruille promised me he'll offer them all the help he can."

Peggy's disappointment was turning in a more positive direction. "I'll be happy to take charge of the art in his studio," she offered. "I already have a few pieces at the gallery. I think a memorial exhibition would be appropriate, with the proceeds going to the family and something to Helena of course. I'll wire them with the proposal."

After thanking Harry warmly for his efforts, Peggy began to envision her gallery's tribute to the late Wifredo Lam. She would have Breton write something for the brochure and borrow the two gouaches, *Mother and Child* and *Satan*, which the Museum of Modern Art's director, Alfred Barr, had acquired for the collection. It was going to be a splendid show.

SEVENTY-TWO.

In O'Connell's office, he and Collins were reviewing the evidence against Solana. They would have to charge him soon or release him back to the Coast Guard for deportation.

"His prints match the ones we found on Lam's mirror," said Collins. "Nice clear dabs, over on the right-hand edge. He must have moved it or tilted it away from the wall while he was looking for the money." In fact those prints had been left on Carlos's previous visit, when he helped Lam reposition the heavy glass.

"What beats me is that he didn't think to search Lam," mused O'Connell. "The cash was right there in his back pocket."

Collins speculated. "Way I see it now, Solana shows up, tries to touch Lam for a loan. They've been down that road before, and Lam knows he's a deadbeat so he refuses. Solana gets mad, beans him, and starts searching, never dreaming that Lam would actually have money on him."

"Go, on, I'm listening," encouraged O'Connell.

"So he looks around for a while—behind the mirror, in the closet, under the mattress, in the dresser drawers— then he realizes Lam ain't moving. Ain't breathing, in fact. Time to beat it, but not before he dresses him up to throw suspicion on his artist pals. By the time we wise up he'll be long gone. And it almost worked."

"It would have worked," O'Connell pointed out, "if that punk up in Harlem hadn't shot his mouth off. What a break that was."

"Good thing for us that Diaz and Morales are on the case."

O'Connell agreed. "Too bad Morales couldn't get Solana to talk, but we have enough circumstantial evidence to charge him. He and Lam were known associates, his prints are in the crib, and we can place him on shore that evening. Have we got the time of death narrowed down, by the way?"

"Rigor mortis had set in by the time the doc got to him," said Collins, "but from the body temperature he doesn't think he'd been dead more than four hours. The French guy found him around 10:30, and we didn't get there until after midnight, so the doc put it around 8:00, 8:30."

"Is he sure it can't be any later?" asked O'Connell, sensing a loose thread that could unravel the case. "The Port Authority guy told me the *Princesa*'s crew was cleared to disembark at 8:45."

"I don't know, but I'll find out," Collins told him. "I think there's some latitude, but let's see what the doc says now that he's done the autopsy."

"Get on it right away. I want to write up the manslaughter charge today. Can't hold him on suspicion much longer."

SEVENTY-THREE.

"Come on, fella. Shake a leg, yer wanted fer the beauty pageant," Sergeant Ryan bellowed into Carlos's cell. He struck the bars with his nightstick. "Chop, chop," he added for emphasis.

Carlos had no idea what Ryan was saying, but he knew an order when he heard one. He stood by the cell door and waited as Ryan unlocked it. The sergeant pulled him out and slammed the gate on the drunk and disorderly that had shared the cell with Carlos last night.

He was marched down the hall to another locked door that opened onto a narrow platform on which several other uncomfortable men were assembled.

"Take off yer beanie." Ryan growled. When he got no response, he yanked off Carlos's watch cap and handed it to him. "Stand over there," he commanded. Again no response, so he manhandled the confused sailor into position in the lineup, where the other men, shuffling and muttering, were being told to stand still, stand up straight, remove their hats, and shut up.

Suddenly, bright lights illuminated the whole platform. A side door opened, and two men and one woman filed in and stood opposite the lineup. Carlos squinted, and despite the glare he recognized the plainclothes policeman,

218

and thought he'd seen the other man before. He could also see that the woman was beautiful. Just for a moment he was heartened. That feeling disappeared as he saw her whisper to the familiar man and then slip back into the shadows. Regardless of the light's intensity, the warmth seemed to drain from the room.

Collins had explained the procedure beforehand. It was entirely up to Breton to make the call. All he needed to do was read the number printed on the wall above the man he recognized. If he couldn't identify Solana or wasn't sure, he should signal Jacqueline and she would interpret.

The process made him deeply uneasy. It smacked of show trials, the kind of bogus prosecutions of which the Nazis were so fond. He almost bolted from the room, but Collins gently steered him up and down the row. He had assured Breton that if he picked Carlos out of the lineup, the man would receive a fair trial in open court and have every opportunity to defend himself. In fact, an attorney would be provided at no cost to him.

Breton stepped back to where Jacqueline was waiting. "He is there. What shall I do?"

"Are you sure?"

"Yes." Breton faced a profound moral dilemma. "If he killed Lam, he should be punished. But perhaps he is innocent. How can I be sure that, if I identify him, he will be justly treated?"

Jacqueline was sympathetic. They both had too much experience of duplicity and corruption to take the authorities at their word.

The only French Collins knew was déjà vu, but a little birdie told him that Breton had spotted the guy and was having misgivings. He decided to let it ride.

Jacqueline took her husband's arm and pulled him close. Their marriage was unraveling, but they shared a past that neither her feelings for David nor his resentment of her infidelity could erase. On the deepest level—beneath the intellectual, the artistic, even the carnal—they trusted each other.

"We are in the new world, André. We have left the evil behind. We must believe that the good is here, and that it will triumph. This is a test of that belief."

He touched her cheek. "Do you believe it?"

"Yes."

Breton turned, and together they approached Collins.

"Trois," he whispered to Jacqueline. "Il est numéro trois." She translated.

SEVENTY-FOUR.

By the time he reached Matta's apartment, Hare was winded. He had sprinted all the way from his loft and had just enough breath left to blurt out, "They've got Carlos!"

"For Christ's sake, keep your voice down," Matta warned him as he led him into the studio. "Anne is asleep. She hasn't been herself since I told her Lam was dead. She had a bad feeling about Carlos when he came here on Sunday night, maybe it was women's intuition, but I think she suspected he was a problem. My story confirmed it." He closed the studio door.

"Who's got Carlos?"

"The police. Here. They must have intercepted the ship and taken him off."

The studio was warm, but Matta felt a cold chill. "How is that possible? How in God's name did they find him?"

Hare shook his head. "I have no idea. All I know is that he's being held at the 6th Precinct. I found out from Jacqueline. That detective, Collins, went to see Breton again. She had to translate. Collins wanted to know if André could recognize Solana. He said yes, he'd met him a couple of times, when Lam brought him along to our gatherings. Collins asked if he'd seen him anywhere near

Lam's apartment on Saturday night. André said he wasn't sure. So Collins asked him to go down to the station and try to pick him out of a lineup. That's how Jacqueline found out he's in custody. She called me right away, all excited because it means the police have their man and he's not one of us."

Matta was thinking furiously. "My story still holds up," he said. "There's nothing to link us to Carlos. Unless he talks."

"Why wouldn't he talk?" Hare was being realistic. "If they charge him with Lam's murder, he'll claim he had no reason to kill him because they were partners in the smuggling racket. He'll say somebody else robbed him and killed him before he got there. They may not believe him, but he'll probably expose you as their silent partner. You told him you arranged it."

Hare had a sudden thought.

"He doesn't know about me, but of course, you do."

Matta stared at him in disbelief. "What are you saying, David? Surely you don't think I'd implicate you?"

"Where did you get the front money? They're sure to ask you that."

"I could have borrowed it from you without telling you why I needed it. Jesus, what do you take me for?"

Hare was disgusted with himself. Matta had his character flaws—smug. self-centered. look at the way he treated Anne—and clearly he was capable of deceit, but of informing on a friend? He was ashamed even to have implied it.

"Please forgive me. I didn't realize how that sounded. I would never think . . ."

His apology was cut short as the studio door opened and Anne entered the room. Hare started to rise and excuse himself.

"Sit down, David." she demanded, with more energy than Matta had seen in her for some time. "I was

222

wide awake when you came in, and I heard what you said."
Her gaze turned toward her husband. "I've been listening
outside the door ever since you closed it."

As she moved into the room, her body appeared to
stiffen with resolve. Both men felt oddly immobilized by
her presence, at a loss for words and incapable of action.
They simply sat and waited for her to continue.

When she spoke, her voice strained to control her
pent-up emotion.

"There's something you need to know."

Thursday afternoon

SEVENTY-FIVE.

Back in his cell——alone now, since the drunk and disorderly had been sprung——Carlos signaled the guard.

"Por favor, señor, ven aquí." Sticking his arm through the bars, he waved Francisco Ortiz's card.

The guard ambled over. "So, changed yer mind, have ya?" He took the card. "You sit tight now, don't go away," he mocked. "You'd better hope this shyster has a magic wand, 'cause that's what it's gonna take to get you off."

Two hours later, Carlos was again sitting opposite Ortiz in the interview room. The attorney opened his notebook and reviewed the notes from his briefing with O'Connell.

"They are charging you with the voluntary manslaughter of Wifredo Lam. Do you know what that means?" he asked. Carlos shook his head.

"It means that either you attacked him intending to kill him or you intended to inflict bodily harm that resulted in his death. It is a lesser charge than murder, which assumes premeditation—in other words, that you went there deliberately to kill him."

"I swear by all that is holy. I never touched him until after he was dead. How can I make you believe me?"

Ortiz gave Carlos a hard look. "You can start by explaining why you didn't go to the police when you found the body, why you assumed someone killed him, and why you tried to place the blame on one of his artist friends."

Carlos jumped directly to the second question. "I suppose he could have had a bad heart or some kind of fit that killed him, but I thought he had been robbed. I got scared. I was afraid someone would accuse me."

"Why would anyone do that?"

"Because I am a foreigner. I speak no English, and I was often at his place."

"If someone robbed him, what would they have stolen? From what the police told me, the only valuable things he owned were still in the apartment."

"Money. He had money there."

"The money was still in his pocket."

Carlos gasped. "You say he was not robbed?"

"He was not," Ortiz informed him. "The police believe you went there to ask him for a loan because, as you say, you knew he had money. But you didn't think he would have it on him. He refused and you knocked him out so you could search the place. They know you were there, they found your fingerprints. But you hit him too hard, killed him, and tried to send the cops in the wrong direction until you could get away. That's their case."

Carlos came to a decision. "You told me yesterday that what I say to you is private, between you and me only. No police." He looked searchingly at Ortiz. "Is that really true?"

The attorney understood his dilemma. "I know it is hard to believe, but yes, it is true. What you and I say here goes no further, unless you allow it."

"Then I will tell you why I was there, and why I did not call the police when I found Lam dead. Why I made the body into an exquisite corpse."

225

"A what?" Ortiz thought he had misheard *cadáver exquisito*. The police had not gone into detail about the nature of the costume, only that it was an inside joke among Lam's artist friends.

Carlos explained what it meant. And he told Ortiz about the drug deal. "That is why I could not go to the police. I still had the parcel."

"What did you do with it?"

"I sold it to a man in Harlem. He gave me $500. The money is on the *Princesa*, under my bunk."

The complications were becoming clear to Ortiz. He could appreciate why Carlos would try to implicate someone else and was rather impressed by his ingenuity. He needed the answer to one more question.

"What made you think of using the exquisite corpse costume?"

"I thought one of the Surrealists killed him."

"That is what I think, too," replied Ortiz.

SEVENTY-SIX.

The intercom buzzed on Detective Collins's desk.

"Yes, Joe, what is it?"

"There's a lady out here, says she wants to see you about the Lam killing. Says her name is Mrs. Roberto Matta."

Collins's curiosity was aroused. "Bring her to my office."

When Sergeant Ryan opened the door, Collins greeted a nervous but resolute Anne Matta. He saw a woman in her late twenties, not exactly beautiful but strikingly good-looking. He was impressed by the graceful way she carried herself, her dark lustrous hair, and delicate slightly elfin features—qualities that had inspired the experimental filmmaker Maya Deren to cast Anne in her Surrealist-inspired movie, "Witch's Cradle." Filmed at Art of This Century, Anne drifted through the galleries like a sleepwalker, encountering fantastic sculptures while Marcel Duchamp made cat's cradles and was throttled by some of the very string he was playing with.

Anne introduced herself and accepted Collins's offer of a chair opposite his desk. This is going to be interesting, he thought. I wonder if she's going to reinforce her husband's story, or contradict it.

She was composed but wound tight with anticipation. She knew very well what she was going to say—she, Roberto, and David had gone over it enough times last night—but she had never before deliberately lied to anyone in authority. Even as a child, she was not given to fibbing to her parents or teachers. She believed in owning up and taking your medicine.

But this was different. You're not a kid any more, she told herself, you have a husband and children to consider. She adjusted her posture, looked Collins straight in the eye, and said, "I understand you have a man in custody for the Lam killing."

"Yes, ma'am, that's right."

"He didn't do it," she said. "I did."

That was certainly not what Collins was expecting to hear. For a moment he simply stared back at her, unsure of how to proceed. He cleared his throat.

"Mrs. Matta, you have just admitted to a very serious offense. You're entitled to a lawyer, who may advise you not to say anything more, because what you say could be used against you in court."

Anne reassured him. "I'm aware of my legal rights, Mr. Collins. My father is an attorney. I would like to make a formal statement."

"I'll get the stenographer in here," he said. She nodded her agreement. He buzzed through to the clerk, who presently entered the room with his stenotype machine.

Once the clerk indicated that he was ready to begin, Collins asked Anne to state and spell her full name and to repeat what she had told him a few moments ago.

"I killed Wifredo Lam," she declared. Her voice was flat, not at all emotional, but Collins sensed that she was struggling to control her feelings.

This was the hardest part for her. Not only was she confessing to what she believed was a crime, but she was also about to make a false statement to a police officer. If

228

she had to repeat it under oath in court, she would be guilty of perjury.

"In Paris, before I met Roberto, Fredo and I were lovers. Then I fell in love with Roberto, and I broke it off." She waved her hand as if to swat away a bad memory. "He and Helena found each other, so he moved on, too."

Her hand returned to her lap. "Helena Holzer," she explained, "a German woman living in Paris. She's some kind of scientist. She was working in a lab there. I think they met through Max Ernst, one of Fredo's artist friends. He's German, too.

"When the war came, Roberto and I got out just in time. A couple of years later, I learned that Fredo and Helena had gotten away and were living in Cuba. Many of our friends were not so fortunate, but with help some of them were able to escape. Fredo was among the lucky ones. I was so relieved and my affection for him, well, I was reminded of it."

Anne cast her eyes down, in what Collins interpreted as a gesture of embarrassment. "I wrote to him, rather indiscreetly, I'm afraid, but I thought I'd never see him again."

She hesitated, and for a moment it seemed she might break off her narrative. Just as Collins wondered if he might have to prompt her, she continued.

"Then, last fall, he suddenly appeared in New York, alone. Helena was still in Cuba. At first I was delighted to see him safe and well, but I soon found out that he wanted to resume our affair. Apparently my letters had encouraged him. By that time I was pregnant, and in any case I was married to Roberto, so I told him no.

"He left me alone until after the twins were born," she brightened momentarily, "our two beautiful boys, Sebastian and Gordon, they were born in June." Her smile faded. "But then he started up again. He was persistent. He threatened to show Roberto my letters."

So, Collins silently confirmed, this is a sex case after all. "And that scared you?" he encouraged.

"I was afraid he'd ruin everything. Roberto is very possessive. So I decided to confront Fredo, try to get the letters back. But it was hard to find the right time, what with the boys to take care of, so I arranged a visit to my parents in Connecticut."

Here Anne relaxed just a bit, since she was transitioning from fiction to a story based on what actually happened. Not the whole truth, to be sure—in her telling, love letters would take the place of cocaine—but closer to reality than she had been so far.

"On Saturday morning, I left the twins with Mother, took the train into the city, and went to Fredo's apartment. I thought we could discuss the situation like adults, but he became unreasonable. I asked for the letters and he refused."

She lowered her eyes again and, for the first time, looked distressed.

"He . . . he assaulted me. He tried to, you know . . ."

"I understand, Mrs. Matta, you don't have to paint a picture for me." Collins immediately regretted his inappropriate figure of speech, but Anne seemed not to notice the artistic allusion.

"We struggled. I managed to twist out of his arms, and as I did I pushed him off balance. He tripped against the hearthstone and fell back. I heard a thud, more like a crack, really. He must have hit his head against the mantle piece. He just crumpled to the floor. He was out cold. You'll think me heartless, Mr. Collins, but I saw my chance to get the letters. So instead of tending to Fredo I searched for the letters and I found them."

Matta and Hare had been insistent on her having a reason to go through the apartment that didn't involve looking for drugs. A search for love letters would account for any fingerprints.

"I heard him groan, and I thought he was coming around so I left. I went home to my parents' house. I was only gone a few hours. I told them I went window-shopping in Darien and walked in the park, just for a break. I burned the letters, and I thought that would be the end of it, but now I find out that he died from that hit on the head."

"How do you know that?' asked Collins. He kept his tone neutral, not challenging, just curious.

"Well, didn't he?" she replied. "Bob Motherwell told David you said it was a hit on the head that killed him. And I did it. I pushed him, he fell and hit his head, and later he died."

"That was five days ago, Mrs. Matta," Collins reminded her. "Why didn't you come forward sooner?"

They had anticipated that question during the rehearsal.

"I only found out he was dead last night. Roberto wasn't going to tell me at all, but I overheard him and David talking about it in the studio when they didn't know I was listening." She looked vaguely annoyed. "I don't know how he thought I wouldn't find out sooner or later. I guess he wanted it to be as later as possible, after it was all cleared up."

Her eyes fixed firmly on Collins. "Of course he had no idea it was my fault. But when I heard them say that someone had been arrested for the crime, I could hardly stand by and let an innocent man go to jail, or worse, for something I did."

"So they told you about this Solana fella we have in custody?"

"Yes. They said André identified him." A look of disgust crossed her face. "They said he dressed Fredo up like an exquisite corpse to throw suspicion on one of his artist friends. What a horrible thing to do! Humiliating. And cowardly. He must have been desperate."

"I think you're right there, ma'am. He was afraid he'd be fingered as the killer, and sure enough he was. He's the logical suspect."

Anne tried to draw him out, to find out if he knew anything about the drug deal, and who was in it with Lam and Solana.

"Why would he want to kill Fredo?" she asked.

"We thought he tried to tap him for a loan and clocked him when he said no," Collins explained. "But from what you say, it looks like he's telling the truth. Lam was dead when he got there. What time did you say you, ah, struggled with him?"

Anne was ready for this. "I took the 10:05 from Darien to Grand Central, then the subway downtown. I think I got to Fredo's at about half past 11:00, and left before noon. There was a 12:30 back to Darien, and I caught it."

SEVENTY-SEVEN.

Collins excused himself and went out to the front desk.

"Is Frank Ortiz still in there with Solana?" he asked Sergeant Ryan.

"Yeah. You want I should get him?"

"No, not yet. I want to talk to him before he leaves, but I gotta talk to O'Connell first. Just don't let him go until I see him."

On his way to O'Connell, he popped his head back in his office, where Anne sat quiet and composed, and the clerk was packing up his equipment.

"I'm going to ask you to wait in the hall while Jeff here types up your statement," he told her. "We'll come back in when it's done, and you can review it. Meanwhile, if you want a lawyer, you can use the phone at the front desk. Sergeant Ryan will show you."

"Thank you, Mr. Collins," she replied. She rose and followed him out to the waiting area by the desk. She's a cool customer, he thought. Really got hold of herself, but she's wound pretty tight. Must have been a shock finding out her old flame wanted to light the fire again, and he's willing to blackmail her to get her into bed. And her with a husband and kids!

233

"Come," barked O'Connell in reply to Collins's knock. He entered, took his customary seat beside the desk, and gave his boss a rundown of the conversation with Anne.

"Think she's telling the truth?"

"It's real plausible. She can't produce the letters, says she burned them, and it looks like she was away that weekend. She wasn't home on Sunday morning when I questioned Matta, and he told me she was out of town. We can check the Saturday train times from Darien and confirm that she was out of her folks' house when she said she was. Maybe she still has the ticket stubs, though she probably burned those, too. The conductor might remember her. I expect we'll find that some of the unidentified prints in Lam's place are hers."

"There were some on the galoshes and the chicken's foot, but the only other clear prints on the exquisite corpse items belonged to Lam," said O'Connell. "If Carlos dressed him up, he must have worn gloves. By the way," he continued, "did you find out whether the doc could narrow down the time of death?"

"Not yet. I left a message for him to call me." Collins rose. "I'd better get back to the office and have Anne Matta sign her statement. Should be typed up by now."

"Well," said O'Connell, "after you do that, we ought to have a talk with Ortiz."

SEVENTY-EIGHT.

Escorting Anne back into his office, Collins speculated silently on her motive for coming forward. He couldn't put his finger on it, but he had a feeling her story wasn't entirely true. He tried to dismiss his doubts, partly because he sympathized with her and partly because it made perfect sense the way she laid it out.

He also realized that his misgivings were caused by his personal dislike of her husband. Matta had rubbed him the wrong way from the start. Covering up something, in his opinion. So now maybe the wife was covering up for him.

Suppose Matta found out that Lam was putting the make on her? She said he was possessive. Suppose he went over to Lam's to have it out? Suppose it was him, not Anne, who got into a shoving match with the guy? Or even bashed his head on purpose? She could be lying to protect him.

After she was seated opposite him, Collins buzzed the desk.

"Is Jeff finished transcribing Mrs. Matta's statement?" he asked.

"Not yet," said Ryan, who turned away from the intercom and shouted into the office. A muffled reply was audible. "He says he's almost done. You want I should buzz you when it's ready?"

"Yeah, do that," he grumbled, still trying to shake that nagging doubt. He looked up to find Anne staring absently out the window at the brick wall opposite. If she's nervous, she sure ain't showing it, he thought. And if she's a liar, she's a real pro. Couldn't have been more sincere if she was in the confessional. Maybe I'm just too suspicious. And if she sticks to her story, who's gonna contradict her?

The phone on his desk rang.

"It's the doc on the line," Ryan told him. "I said you had someone with you, so he knows you can't say much."

"Put him on," said Collins. "Excuse me a moment, Mrs. Matta. Your statement will be ready in a few minutes."

"That's all right, Mr. Collins," she replied evenly, apparently not perturbed by the delay. She just sat patiently and waited, showing no curiosity about his caller.

Collins greeted Dr. Helpern with a neutral hello. "Thanks for returning my call. Do you have the information I asked for?"

"Yes. I can confirm that Lam was dead by 8:30 p.m., no later. Rigor doesn't set in until three hours after death, and he was already stiff by the time I got there just after midnight."

Solana was still on the ship at 8:30, so he'd be in the clear even if Anne Matta hadn't come forward. But her admission also cleared any other potential suspects.

Collins thanked Helpern again and hung up. He decided to fill the waiting time by trying to get Anne to elaborate on the background of her relationship with Lam. Maybe he could plug the hole he perceived in her story.

"You said you and Lam had an affair in Paris, is that right?"

"Yes," she replied somewhat wistfully, "I was very young." What she was actually recalling was her

236

infatuation with Roberto, the romantic early days of their relationship. "Everyone knew war was coming," she continued, "and, being foreigners, we both knew we could be in danger. It made us fearful, but it was exciting, too. I know that sounds foolish, and I don't expect you to understand."

Collins regarded her with sympathy—even, he had to admit, a tinge of envy. It had been a long time since he had felt the kind of sexual passion she was describing, not in so many words but by intimating the emotions that are heightened by anxiety. Knowing you may be parted at any moment, never to see one another again, hones a uniquely sharp edge on lovemaking.

A knock on the door rescued him from further imaginings.

The clerk entered and placed the typed statement on the desk in front of Anne.

"Please read this," Collins instructed, "and initial any changes or corrections you want to make before you sign it."

She glanced at the typescript, signed it, and handed it to Collins. Her haste was the first indication that she was eager for the ordeal to be over.

They both stood, and Collins reached across the desk to shake her hand. Her grasp was steady but her hand seemed fragile, and he took care to be gentle as he thanked her for coming forward.

"On the face of it," he said, "this is a case of accidental death. I'm not a lawyer, mind you, but I think you won't be charged with a criminal offense. If I'm right, you won't even have to go to court. It'll be settled at a coroner's inquest."

To his surprise, she showed no relief. In fact she hardly reacted at all. It was as if she were prepared for whatever the outcome of her confession was, and ready to take the consequences. Innocent, responsible, culpable, guilty—it was all the same to her, or so it seemed.

"Please release the man you're holding," she said earnestly. "He had nothing to do with Fredo's death."

Collins told her that she had cleared him, but it was really the medical examiner's information that had done the trick.

SEVENTY-NINE.

Collins knocked on the interview room door and interrupted Ortiz's conference with his client. "See you a minute, Frank?" he asked. They stepped into the hall. "Come to my office, will you? I have something you need to look at." A uniform appeared and stationed himself inside the door that he locked behind Ortiz. "What's up?" the lawyer asked as they walked.

"I just had a real interesting visitor," Collins told him, "the wife of one of Lam's artist friends. She made a statement I think you should read."

Settled behind his desk, with Ortiz opposite, Collins offered him a cigarette and Anne's typed statement. Ortiz accepted both, and they smoked silently while he read. He went through it twice, stubbed out his cigarette, and nodded his head.

"Without disclosing anything my client told me in confidence," he said, "this corroborates his story. If this is true—and I don't suppose you have any reason to doubt her account—Lam sustained his injury around noon."

"The M.E. says he was definitely dead by 8:30. Must have done a slow bleed inside his skull, wouldn't show on the outside. He probably thought he'd be okay, didn't realize how serious it was. After a few hours he just collapsed, didn't wake up."

239

Ortiz nodded in agreement. "Solana told me he found him dead at 9:00 or thereabouts."

"In fact, that's the earliest he could have gotten there," said Collins. "He wasn't cleared to leave the ship until a quarter to."

"Looks like the case against him just evaporated," remarked Ortiz with satisfaction. He hadn't been looking forward to representing Solana with nothing but his denial as a defense.

Collins agreed. "I guess we can drop the charges, all right. But I want you to get his account for the record. His relationship to Lam, his movements while he was on shore, how he rigged up the exquisite corpse outfit. I want that all in English—signed, sealed and delivered—before I spring him."

"I'll take care of it," said Ortiz. "When you cut him loose, I'll arrange lodging for him at the Seamen's Church Institute until his ship comes back to New York in a couple of weeks. He'll be available for the inquest. You let me know when and where, and I'll be there to translate for him. The Coast Guard has nothing on him, so after that he should be free to go."

"Thanks for handling this, Frank. I'll notify Morales up at the 23rd. He and Officer Diaz have been in the lead on this case. Actually, they're the ones who identified Solana."

"What about Lam's family in Cuba? Do they know he's dead?"

"I cabled them on Tuesday, care of the embassy in Havana, but it turns out they already knew. Apparently his art dealer has a contact there, and she told them. I'll keep them informed about the inquest and the verdict."

"You're confident that the coroner will rule accidental death?"

"If Anne Matta sticks to her story, I don't see what else he can do."

240

Friday night, October 22

EIGHTY.

From his usual perch at the far end of the Agozar's bar, Joey Ramierz could scan the whole room. Idly twirling a silver dollar on the counter, working on his second Bacardi and lime, he was on the lookout for Esperanza, his most popular and lucrative whore, who was due to turn over last night's take. But when he saw Juanita Diaz, dressed in street clothes and arriving with an escort, he cursed silently, polished off his drink, pocketed the coin, and slipped out through the kitchen.

Luis, the owner and bartender, greeted the couple warmly in English since it was obvious that her date was not Hispanic. "Always a pleasure to see you, Nita, especially when it's not official."

She introduced Fitz and mentioned that he had worked with her to crack the Lam case. Word was out that the sailor had been arrested, which meant that the smuggling scheme had gone south. Luis was among the many in Spanish Harlem who were delighting in Joey's misfortune.

"You just missed Joey," Luis reported with a grin. "He spotted you and beat it out the back way."

"Gee, that's too bad," Nita replied, returning his smile. "I guess he's not feeling sociable tonight. I wonder why."

She dismissed Joey from her thoughts and turned her attention to the evening ahead. "I want to treat Fitz to a real Cuban meal," she told Luis, who informed her that her money was no good in the Agozar tonight.

"Dinner is on the house," he insisted over her protests, escorting them to a cozy table for two in a softly lighted corner. "What are you drinking?" he asked.

"Let's have a couple of Hatueys," she suggested. "Santiago pale ale to go with authentic Cuban food." Fitz readily agreed.

"Thank goodness my cook is to old for the draft," said Luis. "My waiters are all gone. I have to rely on my son Pepe, that skinny kid over there." He pointed to a very busy teenager shuttling among the tables. "Call him when you're ready to order. I'll bring your beers."

The menu was on a chalkboard on the wall. Nita translated.

"Are you observant? If so, go for the bacalao con papas. That's codfish with potatoes. Otherwise, the arroz con pollo, chicken and rice, is excellent."

"What about you?" he wondered. "Do you do the fish on Friday routine?"

Nita laughed. A warm, throaty sound that made Fitz's ears tingle. "I'm lapsed," she admitted. "Haven't been to church in years. I hope you're not shocked."

Actually, he was delighted. "I go with the family, but my heart's not in it. I don't know why, maybe it's the state of the world that makes it hard for me to have faith." Suddenly serious, he looked at Nita earnestly. "Hard to think about the future, too, you know? If this war drags on, I might find myself in a different uniform."

Luis arrived with their Hatueys at an opportune moment, interrupting a mood that threatened to dampen their celebration. Smiling broadly as he poured the beers, he told them, "Take your time, no rush," and deposited a breadbasket on the table.

Fitz apologized. "I should never have brought it up," he said. "If it happens, it happens. Anyway, it's not happening tonight."

Nita leaned across the table and took his hands in hers. She locked eyes with him.

"I'll tell you what *is* happening tonight. We're going to get slightly tipsy, enjoy a delicious meal, and walk back to my place. I'm going to make coffee, and then we're going to make love."

Her eyes twinkled. "Are you shocked now?"

That was putting it mildly. Fitz was flabbergasted. Dumbfounded. Floored. Speechless. He felt the blood rush to his head. His mouth opened but nothing came out.

Nita giggled. "Fitz, you're blushing."

When words finally came to him, all he could think of to say was, "Your mother?"

"Visiting my aunt in the Bronx. She'll be gone all weekend."

They skipped the coffee.

Later, when they lay wrapped in each other's arms, he asked her if there was anyone else, maybe some guy overseas. Having just demonstrated that she was no virgin, she said that she wouldn't be writing a Dear John letter to a serviceman. "How about you?" she wanted to know. He told her about Mary Dolan, now engaged to a navy pilot and out of his life.

Fitz ran his fingers through Nita's tousled hair as she nestled against his naked shoulder.

"I'm crazy about you," he confessed. "How did this happen so fast? Not even a week, and I already know I want to marry you. Do you want to marry me?"

She sighed and nodded. "We're both crazy. Two cops, what a pair we'll make."

She propped herself on an elbow and frowned at him. "I'm not going to quit the force, understand? No kids, not for a while anyway. Forget the rhythm method, you'll use protection like you did just now." A handy vending machine in the Agozar's men's room had made a stop at the drugstore unnecessary.

Fitz rolled his eyes. "Laying down the law already? Well, Officer Diaz, you'd better take me into custody."

And she did.

EIGHTY-ONE.

The inquest didn't take long. The presence of Anne's respectable-looking parents, each one holding an adorable infant, made a favorable impression. The medical examiner's evidence established the cause of death, Detective Sergeant O'Connell described the investigation, and the only other witnesses, Anne and Carlos, reiterated their formal statements. Neither one mentioned the aspects of their stories that either disguised or contradicted the truth—Carlos never disclosed his drug smuggling deal, and Anne neglected to explain that her knowledge of that crime was what led her to visit Lam on the fateful Saturday. Their accounts were accepted, and the cause of death was ruled to be accidental.

As Matta led his wife from the coroner's office, with the Clarks forming a protective escort, he glanced menacingly at Carlos, who was being shepherded by Francisco Ortiz. Feeling the animosity, Carlos looked away quickly. He could hardly blame Matta and regretted his creation of the exquisite corpse, but now it was over and he was free.

Or was he? What about his deal with Joey Ramirez? He waited until he and Ortiz were in the corridor, away from Matta, who could understand their conversation.

"Are you still my lawyer?" he asked.

"That is up to you," replied Ortiz. "Do you need further counsel?"

"I told you about the deal with Ramirez," said Carlos. Ortiz nodded. "He paid me $500. I am supposed to pay $150 to the man in Cartagena for more cocaine. If I do not go through with it, what will happen to me when I return to New York? He could want to punish me for taking his front money."

Ortiz understood his problem. "That is why you are going to pay him back. If you return his outlay, he has no reason to retaliate. He bought the drugs from you, so that part is yours, and when the *Princesa* returns it should still be under your bunk. How much money is in your Seamen's Bank account?"

"My wages for the last trip, $175, plus some from before. A couple of hundred, I guess." With a free berth at the institute, he had been living on what was left of the broken fifty.

"Good," said Ortiz. "You and I will go there and you will draw out $150 in cash. I will get the money to Ramirez. I have no doubt he already knows you were arrested and charged—I am sure Detective Morales took care of that. He suspected there was a smuggling deal behind the whole business. Getting word to Ramirez will put him on notice that the police are wise to him, so he will have to back off. And of course they will be watching you, so you will have to stay clean."

Carlos was listening carefully. "Does that mean I will not be able to bring in any more Cuban cigars?"

Ortiz chuckled. "Mr. Solana, the answer is yes. On the advice of counsel, you have just decided to go straight."

Tuesday evening, November 30

EIGHTY-TWO.

The opening reception at Art of This Century for "Wifredo Lam: A Memorial Exhibition" had attracted a distinguished crowd. In addition to the full complement of refugee Surrealists—even the despised Dalí and the apostate Masson had turned up—and the young Americans itching to take their places at the head of the vanguard, Peggy had recruited some serious collectors. A personal call to each of them ensured their attendance.

"I'm not taking a commission on sales," she told them. "All the proceeds will go to Lam's family. And of course his prices will soon rise now that he's dead," she added with practical wisdom, "so you really must take advantage of this opportunity." Her blandishments had lured Saidie May from Baltimore and Edna Winston from Detroit, as well as the New York collectors Sidney Janis, who would soon retire from the clothing business and open his own art gallery, and Nelson Rockefeller, whose mother was a founder of the Museum of Modern Art.

Standing beside Peggy as she proudly surveyed the turnout was Alfred Barr, the museum's embattled former director, who had approved the loan of the two Lam gouaches just prior to being sacked. In a long-running battle of wills with the Modern's dictatorial president, his enthusiasm for the more radical types of modernism had cost him the top job. But his supporters had rallied and he had been kept on to oversee his first love, the permanent collection.

Barr remarked on the odd mixture of art-world regulars and outsiders.

"Who are those two young redheads holding hands and looking confused?" he asked her. "A handsome couple, but not among your clients, I assume."

"The police," she replied, enjoying his shocked reaction. "And there are several other officers of the law here tonight as well." She gestured across the room.

"See that large black-haired gentleman over there, talking to the lady who looks like a gypsy? He's the detective who broke the Lam case. And the lady is Madame Carmen, a genuine gypsy fortune-teller from Spanish Harlem. She knew before anyone else that a woman was involved. According to Officer Fitzgerald—he's the red-haired policeman, a charming young fellow—Madame Carmen had only to touch the photograph of Lam's body to sense a woman's aura. Isn't it thrilling?"

"Surely you don't believe in such hocus-pocus."

"I never did before, but now I wonder," she admitted. "Officer Fitzgerald told me they went to her because they thought the way Lam's body was decked out had something to do with Cuban voodoo. That lovely young woman with him, Officer Diaz—yes, a female police officer, isn't that wonderful—was his interpreter. They were thrown together by the investigation, and look at the result! You can see how much in love they are."

"And how perplexed they are," Barr observed. "Evidently Lam's work is a bit over their heads."

"That's hardly surprising," she pointed out. "I don't suppose they've ever set foot in your museum, much less in a gallery like this one. Not that there's another gallery like it anywhere. The best of both worlds, Europe and America.

I must ask them what they think of the Surrealist collection and the abstract room. I do so enjoy exposing young people to advanced art, as I'm sure you do, too. We must bring along the next generation, mustn't we?"

Barr favored her with an indulgent smile. "Peggy, my dear, you are incorrigible. You don't give a rap for the next generation. Even your own children take second place behind your collection. Sometimes I think you love your paintings more than you do Sinbad and Pegeen."

"What a wicked thing to say, Alfred! I adore the children. Of course, I have neglected them from time to time, especially when I've been romantically involved, but I know they understand. Besides, they love the collection as much as I do. Well, almost as much."

Barr decided on a tactical retreat. "As you say. And it's good of you to encourage Pegeen's artistic efforts. Her painting in your show of female artists last winter was charming."

"Thirty-One Women," Peggy recalled ruefully, "one woman too many. Dorothea Tanning, that vulgar little minx, set her cap for Max and now he chases after her like a lovesick teenager. I have to admit she's a good painter, but I curse the day I put her in the show.

"And there they are," she nodded toward her husband and his lover, who were at the center of a scrum of Max's admirers on the other side of the room. "He has the nerve to parade her right under my nose."

Fortunately, Peggy's cousin Harry spotted her before she could make a scene.

"A wonderful tribute to Cuba's most important modern artist," he enthused. "I confess I wasn't familiar with his work, but of course he was in Europe when I was posted to Havana. His death is a great loss—to the art world in general and Cuba in particular. But this show will certainly enhance his posthumous reputation."

Harry scanned the gallery. "I see a few potential buyers. As a matter of fact, I think I may be one myself. I've taken a fancy to that large gouache, the jungle scene. Isn't that his last painting?"

"Yes," replied Peggy, effectively diverted from the indiscreet Max. "The last one he finished, that is. There was a companion piece in progress on his easel when he died. That unfinished one, of course, is not for sale."

Always alert to a potential acquisition but woefully short of purchase money, Barr intervened. "I say, Harry, how would you like to buy it for the museum? As a gesture of inter-American good will from the former ambassador to the country where he served with such distinction?"

"My word, Barr, you should be in the diplomatic corps. What do you think, Peggy? Is that a good idea?"

"It's a marvelous idea," she agreed. "And such a boost to his family. I'll have Jimmy put a red dot on the label right away and spread the word that *The Jungle* is going to the Modern's collection."

She winked. "I know that will encourage the others to open their wallets."

EIGHTY-THREE.

"Such mixed feelings," said Motherwell to the knot of Americans clustered around him. "I certainly didn't mind putting off my own show in favor of this one, but I hate to see the word 'memorial' on the invitation and the brochure. Even now, it's hard to believe he's gone."

"Look at the crowd," said Baziotes, spotting Rockefeller now in conversation with Peggy and Barr. "There's some money in the room, for sure."

"A lot of strangers, too," observed Rosenberg. "I recognize the police commissioner, but only from his picture in the paper. I've certainly never seen him here before."

Motherwell laughed. "That's because you don't buy tickets to any of Peggy's benefit events. He's a family friend of the Guggenheims, so she ropes him in whenever she's raising money for one of her causes."

Rosenberg didn't like being reminded that his job at the Office of War Information paid just enough to keep the wolf from the door. Motherwell, subsidized by his father, could afford those tickets, but they were beyond Rosenberg's reach.

"My war work is contribution enough," he grumbled, changing the subject. "I'm surprised to see Matta here, considering that his wife was responsible. Not

251

deliberately, of course, but still . . ." His heavy brows frowned in disapproval.

"I had no idea she was involved with Lam before she married Matta," said Kamrowski. "Too bad he carried a torch. Hard to blame him though, she's a sweet little number. Turned out to be his unlucky one."

"Don't be flippant," scolded Motherwell. He decided to show his support for Matta in what must be an uncomfortable situation.

"Very decent of you to come," he said as he shook Matta's hand, pointedly in full view of Rosenberg, Kamrowski, and the others he had just left.

"I promised Pajarito I'd be here," Matta explained. "She obviously couldn't come herself. She wanted everyone to know that I don't blame her. It might look otherwise if I stayed away."

Motherwell could appreciate the reasoning. He also assumed that Matta must have known about Anne and Fredo in Paris—an affair that, while it never happened, was now common knowledge, as were its fatal consequences. Like Collins, he wondered if Anne had taken the blame for her husband's jealous outburst.

He banished that thought to the back of his mind. Whether Roberto or Anne had pushed him, Lam's death was an accident. That was the official verdict.

EIGHTY-FOUR.

O'Connell and Collins stood together in a corner of the gallery surveying the crowd with practiced eyes. In spite of their civilian clothes, they might as well have had their detective shields pinned to their lapels. Their acumen failed them only when they tried to size up Lam's paintings.

"What do you make of this stuff, Jacko?" asked Collins with off-duty familiarity. "Personally, it gives me the heebie-jeebies."

"You said it, Pat," O'Connell replied. "Especially since every time I look at that big one, with all the boogey men and the plants that look like they could strangle you, I see Lam with his head in a scary mask and a rubber chicken's foot on his leg."

"Seems like somebody bought the thing," said Collins with a grimace. "I think that's what the red spot on the wall next to it means. If I took that home to hang on my wall, my wife would throw it out of the house and me along with it."

He turned his attention back to the gathering. "I see all the artists I interviewed, the yanks and the frogs, including Breton and Duchamp. Even Matta showed up. They're eccentric, all right, but a pretty decent bunch, really cared for Lam. Respected him, too. I'm glad it turned out none of them did him in."

O'Connell regarded him shrewdly. "You sure about that?"

"What I'm sure of," Collins hedged, "is that it was an accident. Case closed. And I'm sure of something else, too."

"Which is?"

"As sure as God made little green apples, them Surrealists are never gonna make another exquisite corpse."

Wifredo Lam, *The Jungle.* 1943
Gouache on paper mounted on canvas, 94 ¼ x 90 ½ inches
The Museum of Modern Art, New York. Inter-American Fund
© 2016 Artists Rights Society (ARS), New York / ADAGP, Paris

AFTERWORD.

Many of the characters in this fictional narrative were real people who lived in New York City in October 1943, when John J. O'Connell (whom I demoted to his earlier rank of Detective Sergeant) was a chief police inspector serving under Police Commissioner Lewis J. Valentine. Milton Helpern, M.D., later known as "The World's Greatest Medical Detective," was the city's deputy chief medical examiner, and Barney Josephson was the proprietor of both Café Society Uptown and Downtown. André Breton was broadcasting for the Voice of America, and Harold Rosenberg was working for the Office of War Information. Peggy Guggenheim was presiding over her gallery, Art of This Century, and her cousin Harry, a former ambassador to Cuba, was the founder and president of *Newsday*. Alfred H. Barr Jr., founding director of the Museum of Modern Art, was fired by the museum's president, Stephen C. Clark, in October, when Lena Horne was in town, appearing with Duke Ellington's orchestra. All the artists who populate the story (but were not involved in drug smuggling) were there, too.

All, that is, except one.

After escaping from Nazi-occupied France in 1941, Wifredo Lam and his lover, Helena Holzer, traveled to Cuba, where he created his most famous painting, *The Jungle*, in his Havana studio in 1943. He and Helena married the following year; they divorced in 1951. After the war, he divided his time among Cuba, France, and the United States, and later established a studio in Italy with the Swedish artist Lou Laurin, whom he married in 1960. Revered as the most distinguished Cuban artist of the twentieth century, he died in Paris in 1982.

MAR 10 2018

CPSIA information can be obtained
at www.ICGtesting.com
Printed in the USA
LVOW10s1151011117
554591LV00002B/450/P